A FAIRY TALE UNMASKED

We would like to thank the following sponsors for their support:

Sparkssen-Stiftung Werra-Meißner. GUTes bewahren-ZUKUNFT gestalten (Savings Bank Foundation Werra-Meißner, Preserving the good-shaping the future), Sparkassen-Kulturstiftung Hessen-Thüringen (Saving Bank Culture Foundation, Hesse-Thuringia) and Landrat des Werra-Meißner-Kreises (District Administrator of the Werra-Meißner district).

A Fairy Tale Unmasked
The Teacher and the Nazi Slaves

PART 1
by D.Z. Stone

based on the work and in cooperation with
Dieter Vaupel

PART 2
by Dieter Vaupel

based on reports and interviews with
Blanka Pudler and translated from German by
Julian Vaupel

VALLENTINE MITCHELL
LONDON • CHICAGO, IL

First published in 2021 by Vallentine Mitchell

Catalyst House,
720 Centennial Court,
Centennial Park, Elstree WD6 3SY, UK

814 N. Franklin Street,
Chicago, Illinois,
IL 60610 USA

www.vmbooks.com

Copyright © 2021 Dieter Vaupel and D.Z. Stone

British Library Cataloguing in Publication Data:
An entry can be found on request

ISBN 978 1 912676 56 9 (Paper)
ISBN 978 1 912676 57 9 (Ebook)

Library of Congress Cataloging in Publication Data:
An entry can be found on request

Contents

Introduction

In 1983, when I was a high school teacher in Hessisch Lichtenau, Germany, students wondered why there were such high levels of TNT and other residues of armament production in the groundwater. We decided to try and find out, and for our school's Project Week we researched the question: What happened to our town during the Nazi regime?

When my students and I asked, we were met with silence, suppression and denial. *We didn't know anything about it! That was so long ago! Let the past finally rest!* But we – my students and the committed citizens of Lichtenau who joined us – said *'No!' We didn't want to let the past go!*

We went on with our research and did not allow ourselves to be intimidated. We uncovered human suffering and were deeply touched by the fate of the 1,000 Jewish girls and women sent to our town from Auschwitz. Finally we looked at how to remember what they had to endure. We did not want to be among those who chose silence, suppression and denial.

What was kept secret in Hessisch Lichtenau was not an isolated case in post-war Germany. After 1945, not only those who took part in the Nazi regime but everyday people who were abused and humiliated during the time of National Socialism wanted to bury what had happened and forget.

Thomas Buergenthal, who survived Auschwitz as a young boy, writes in his memoirs: '…the Holocaust cannot be fully understood if we do not look at it through the eyes of those who have lived through it'.

We tried to do this by putting a face to the individuals on the list of the 1,000 Jewish women and girls sent to Hessisch Lichtenau from Auschwitz: Blanka Pudler, Judith Isaacson, Trude Levi, Kati Salcer and all the others...

We also hoped our research would help warn others so it never happens again. We wanted people to see what can transpire when hatred and intolerance prevail. We hoped people would consider the example of Hessisch Lichtenau and ask if there are people still disregarded due to their culture, religion or other way of life.

We have seen the rise of the right-wing populist party in Germany and in other countries in the past years. We have seen how leading representatives of the German AfD, a right-wing nationalist party, demanded a '180 degree turn' in remembering the Holocaust and described the Holocaust memorial in Berlin as a 'memorial of shame'.

These are warning signs that make us sit up and want people to know that what happened 75 years ago in Hessisch Lichtenau and other places can happen again if we are not vigilant.

Every single person forced to work in the Hessisch Lichtenau munitions factory is a warning to stand up for humanity – a warning not to remain silent and not to look away when someone is attacked, humiliated and violated. To respect and protect human dignity – that is our responsibility.

The example of Hessisch Lichtenau also offers hope for the future. It shows the importance of education and upbringing, what young people can accomplish when they ask questions and refuse to take no for an answer.

Just as schoolchildren got the ball rolling in 1983, today young people are again committed to keeping alive the memory of Blanka Pudler and the other Jewish women and girls. In 2019, inspired by students at the Freiherr-von-Stein-Schule, 2,000 people formed a human chain marking the path the Jewish women and girls were forced to march from the barracks to the factory.

A Fairy Tale Unmasked is written in two parts. In Part I, journalist and author D.Z. Stone tells the story of how we unravelled our town's buried Nazi past and connected with the survivors forced to work in what turned out to have been one of the largest munitions factories in all of Europe.

Part II is an English translation of the memoir of Blanka Pudler published in Germany in 2018, *On a Strange Uninhabitable Planet*. Blanka was a 15-year-old girl when she was sent from Auschwitz to Hessisch Lichtenau to work as a slave labourer. She would return to Germany in later years to tell her story to schoolchildren. For her efforts, in 2012 the German government awarded Blanka the Order of Merit of the Federal Republic of Germany. I am honoured that Blanka let me into her life to work with her on her memoir.

As I promised Blanka before she passed away: 'We will never forget.'

Dieter Vaupel
September 2020

Foreword

A Fairy Tale Unmasked: The Teacher and the Nazi Slaves is two books in one, each building on the other, each enhancing the other. Part I is the effort of a masterful German High school teacher and his innovative and indefatigable students to uncover the true history of their charming town, which had once been the site of a Nazi slave labour camp, something everyone of a certain age in the town knew but chose to forget. Dieter Vaupel shows us how to make history come alive – how to bridge past, present and future, how not only to convey information but to inspire – and the result brings truth and reconciliation to a grim historical reality. Part II is the memoir of Blanka Pudler, who in 1944 was a 15-year-old Hungarian Jewess incarcerated in that camp, posthumously composed from the many times she had told her story when after many years of silence she began to speak. As usual D.Z. Stone writes movingly and compellingly. The result is a story so worth telling, so well told.

The stories are unique yet eerily familiar.

In 1990 I saw a German movie entitled *The Nasty Girl*, which told the story of Anna Rosmus, a young German high school student from Passau who innocently began to research the story of her town believing the stories that had come down to her from her parents and community and from town lore about the manner in which her town and its leadership had not succumbed to the evils of Nazism. Not quite resisters, they treated their local Jews with compassion and solidarity. And then she began her research, reading newspaper clips and archival sources which told a radically different story.

Prominent families in the town had been members of the Nazi Party and the citizens of Passau had participated in the round-up of Jews and their deportation to concentration camps. She has written a prize-winning article and then two well-reviewed, deeply controversial and deeply divisive books shattering the comfortable myths that townspeople had told themselves and others. I met Anna Rosmus after she was forced to leave her hometown and homeland and came to the United States. We hired her at the United States Holocaust Memorial. Working together I heard story after story, so I read of Vaupel and his students with a sense of here it goes again.

Vaupel worked with his students at the same time that Rosmus was doing her work. It was also the moment, some 40 years after the Holocaust – a generation later – when German leadership under Helmut Kohl was wanting to end the post-war period of German shame and put the Holocaust behind them. Many of us can recall the controversy of Bitburg.

Yet, the third generation wants to remember what the second generation chooses to hide and the first generation would prefer to remain in the shadows, forgotten and buried. The truth is difficult to face; therefore ever more important to face. As a teacher, I deeply admire what Vaupel did with his students. He made them active learners. He taught them to understand the importance of history, not only in uncovering the past but also in preparing students to face the future.

Blanka Pudler's story is also a result of the third generation choosing to remember what the second generation wants to forget and what the first generation would prefer to remain in the shadows. She was a survivor who at first was reluctant to remember her past and even more reluctant to transmit it to another generation. But there came a moment in her life when she had to confront her own story and find a way to speak of anguish and death in a manner that enhanced human life, that pleaded for human decency and proclaimed human dignity. Once she did, she became a witness far more than a victim and a symbol of resilience. She faced her demons and her past and made it a tool to contribute to the future. In the second part of this book, her story first told in the classroom is captured on paper, where it shall last.

Imagine also the contribution that Vaupel and his students made to the life of the survivors who bravely came back to the place of their incarceration, only to be told that there never was such a camp, never was such a place, that they don't even remember their own past. When Judith Magyar Isaacson returned in the 1980s, distinctly remembering an underground factory camp, everyone denied her reality. Kati Kellner Salcer, whose biography D.Z. Stone had also written – and to which I contributed a Foreword – was not even believed by her husband, himself a survivor.

Now, thanks to this high school teacher and his enterprising students, the survivors have their past affirmed and the town itself was not permitted to erase its past. Remarkably, facing its past has proved liberating for many townspeople, not only uncovering the evil of the past but the all important and all too rare cases of solidarity and decency, the remnants upon which a different future can be built.

Dieter Vaupel was not forced to leave Germany, but rather he pursued his Ph.D. on the foundation of the research he and his students undertook and continued to teach – this time in higher education – shaping the minds of the third and fourth generation after, understanding so well that the truth must be faced, and if faced with courage and determination can empower a new generation to salvage important lessons from the ashes.

Professor Michael Berenbaum
American Jewish University
Los Angeles, CA

PART I

How a Teacher and his Students Discovered their Town's Hidden Past

1

Something in the Water

In 1975, the picturesque German town of Hessisch Lichtenau, in what was then the Federal Republic of Germany, became a stopover on a new map to promote tourism in the region, the 'Fairy Tale Route'. This 600-kilometer meandering road followed the real lives and mythical stories of the Brothers Jacob and Wilhelm Grimm.

Hessisch Lichtenau, with its half-timbered houses, nearby ruins of Reichenbach Castle, Great Stones purportedly tossed there by giants, and a pond where newborns were said to enter the world, was also home to one of the Brothers Grimm most popular fairy tales, Mother Hulda. The town was nestled at the foot of High Meissner, the mountain where legend held Mother Hulda lived and shook her bed pillows so feathers would fly and snow would fall on the world.

Yet beneath this enchanting façade, all was not idyllic in Hessisch Lichtenau. No one talked about the poison in the water or how it got there.

A year before the Fairy Tale Route was established, in 1974, the local people learned that the authorities had found contaminants in their groundwater, residues of trinitrotoluene from production of the explosive TNT. This information came through one article in the local newspaper, *Hessische Niedersächsische Allgemeine*. What the authorities did not share was how long they had known toxic residues from the wartime production of explosives were in many places over a 250-hectare area near the town.

The first clue came in 1963 when a dog died after falling into an old concrete pool filled with a foul-smelling liquid. It took four years before the first test of the village water supply for contaminants, in 1967. The test showed specific chemical compounds, residues from TNT production, in the drinking water but the public was not informed of any contamination until 1974. After this one mention in the newspaper, no more reports were published on the contamination, and no one talked about the water, at least publicly.

Dieter Vaupel was 29 and a married father with two small children when he came to Hessisch Lichtenau in 1980 to teach history, politics and the German language to the 12-18 year-olds at Freiherr-vom-Stein-Schule, the local high school. At the time, he had never heard of any problem with the

Figure 1: Old City Hall, Market Place, Hessisch Lichtenau 2019. Photo by Tourist Information Hessisch Lichtenau.

town's water. And no one told him about it. What he did get was an inside tip about a good place to swim. Even though there was a 'No Bathing' sign at Hirschhagener Oaks, there was no mention of a reason. So Dieter swam there along with some of his students, and one time with his entire class of 25.

The news of pollutants in the local groundwater only came out in 1982, when the State authorities drilled a new, deeper well for the village water supply several kilometers away from the old well. Vaupel and his students were puzzled – what had happened to their town's water? Where did these poisons from explosive material come from? What happened there during the war?

***

Born in 1950, Dieter Vaupel grew up not far from Hessisch Lichtenau in another story-like landscape, the small town of Spangenberg, population 3,000.

Situated in a valley at the foot of the Schlossberg, a wooded hill leading up from the town to Spangenberg Castle, the area was an adventure playground for Dieter and his older brother Peter, born in 1948. Along with their friends, the brothers spent hours exploring the castle's secret passages and walls, all that was left after the war.

Spangenberg Castle, which held British military during the Second World War, was razed in a bombing raid after the prisoners left. A heartbreaking loss for the townspeople, in the 1950s the State government started to rebuild the castle; it would become a youth hostel and eventually a hotel touted internationally for its fairytale charm and romance.

Dieter credits learning about Spangenberg Castle for promoting his own interest in history – in later years as an academic he would publish articles about the castle. But for his becoming a teacher, he credits his mother.

Always a good student, Martha Holzhauer had to give up her own hope of teaching. After only eight years of schooling she had to quit to work in her family's small butcher shop. However despite marriage and children she did not forget her dream, often telling her son Dieter about it. Thanks to Dieter's father, Karl Vaupel, who worked hard as an insurance agent to support the family, Dieter could attend university and be the first child in the family to fulfil his mother's dream of teaching for her. Dieter's sister Annelie, born in 1953, would follow by also becoming a teacher.

Dieter attended primary school in his hometown and then the Geschwister-Scholl-Schule, a high school in the district town of Melsungen. At a time when talk about the Nazi era was still taboo, he learned about his school's namesakes, Hans and Sophie Scholl. A brother and sister arrested for handing out anti-Nazi leaflets, the siblings were members of The White Rose, a student group engaged in non-violent resistance. In 1943, before they were executed by guillotine at Stadelheim Prison, Sophie Scholl said, 'How can we expect righteousness to prevail when there is hardly anyone willing to give himself up individually to a righteous cause?'

Dieter's interest in the Nazi era was especially piqued by his grandmother Elise Holzhauer. She had a mysterious black handbag full of old pictures and her grandson often sat in her living room with her and looked at them. Elise told stories, and told Dieter about the 100 Jews who had lived in Spangenberg before 1933 with not a single one ever returning.

The town's Jewish butcher, Moses Katz, had slaughtered livestock along with Dieter's butcher grandfather Wilhelm Holzhauer. Years later Dieter would learn that Moses Katz had been arrested by the Nazis for slaughtering

Figure 2: Spangenberg Castle ruins, 1949. Private Archive Dieter Vaupel.

his cattle according to Jewish religious rites. Moses died as a result of the detention. Years later, Dieter Vaupel would write the story of the Spangenberg Jews, detailing their expulsion and murder.

It was during Dieter's last year of high school that students across Germany started turning the country on its head in what would be called the German Student Movement of 1968. A young teacher at Dieter's school who taught history and was completely unlike the typical authoritarian teachers of the time, inspired and shaped Dieter's political interest.

Dieter learned that he no longer had to submit to parents and teachers without asking questions. Like students all over Germany, he and his classmates raised a lot of these, especially about the Nazi past, that could not be asked until then. They wanted to know what really happened and what role their parents and grandparents played. They also stood up for the rights of others, supporting equal opportunities for all and liberation movements across the world.

This new approach to life was also expressed outwardly. Dieter grew his hair long and sported a beard, and as a protest against the consumer-oriented world and the bourgeoisie establishment, wore the cheapest jeans and shirts he could find. Music also played a significant influence, specifically that of Jimi Hendrix, Bob Dylan, Pete Seeger, Joan Baez, John Lennon and Woody Guthrie.

From high school Dieter Vaupel would attend Justus Liebig University Giessen where he would continue to be influenced by the student movement. He would view his work as a teacher in political terms: the goal was to change society and make it more humane through education. His priority would be to work with young people from socially disadvantaged families.

At the end of his university studies Dieter opted for a year of community service as he was sympathetic to the peace movement and refused to serve in the army and train as a soldier. He worked with the organization Social Peace Service, bringing a warm lunch to elderly people who could no longer care for themselves. For many he was the only person they saw; sometimes he would linger for coffee, or walk with them and talk. Following his community service, Dieter began his teaching career in 1977 with his first permanent position at a comprehensive school in Baunatal. In 1980, he and his family would move to his hometown of Spangenberg after he took a position at the local high school in Hessisch Lichtenau.

In 1983, after news came out that the water in Hessisch Lichtenau was being poisoned from residues left over from the production of TNT, Dieter Vaupel's students wanted to know what happened in their town during the war. And he was not afraid to look for answers.

2

Into the Forest

In the spring of 1983, the 1,000 students of the Freiherr-vom-Stein-Schule in Hessisch Lichtenau split up into 50 or so groups for the school's annual Project Week. A widespread practice in German schools, Project Week freed students from regular classes to work on topics they proposed. From arts and culture and natural sciences to practical projects where something was built, the suggested topics were listed and teachers, who led the groups, chose their preferences.

That year, Dieter Vaupel chose to lead the group working on what seemed to be a straightforward question: 'What happened in our town during the Nazi era?' This was a question that may have began over news of the water being poisoned, but like so many young people all over Germany in those years, the students wanted know how their towns and villages lived through the horrors of the Nazi regime.

Little did Dieter imagine how divisive and contentious the topic would be – or how it would alter the trajectory of his life and one day impact a group of Jewish women and girls whose history he could not even imagine.

The first hint of controversy came just after the groups were formed. A boy told Dieter that he had to drop out of the project because his parents said the topic was too dangerous. Then in the weeks leading up to Project Week, the town's resistance became clear when students tried to set up interviews with family members, friends and neighbours. They met a proverbial wall of silence.

Dieter and the students needed to find a way to learn what had happened in Hessisch Lichtenau when no one would talk about it, and there was nothing in the town's written or archival records. They saw the groundwater tainted by TNT residue as a clue and decided to explore the area where the explosives had most likely been produced.

***

Hirschhagen, located in a densely-forested area just outside of Hessisch Lichtenau, had a post-apocalyptic and toxic feel to it. It was an eerie mix of bombed-out and broken-down buildings as well as an active industrial area.

What was not known to Dieter Vaupel and his student group when they began was not only what happened in Hirschhagen during the Nazi era but also right after the war ended. They had no idea that in 1945, buildings on the massive site were dismantled and per the Potsdam Agreement, brought to other countries for reparations. Then about a third of the buildings that remained were blown up.

The rest of the buildings were scheduled to be demolished when the plan was changed by the American military. Some speculate it was the challenge of blowing up reinforced concrete that led to the decision to use the remaining area for industry and refugee settlement. They would house refugees, primarily Germans who fled lands awarded to Poland and Czechoslovakia after the war as well as those from the nearby German Democratic Republic (East Germany).

At the outset of Project Week, Dieter and his students were not completely clueless and knew a few bits and pieces about the area's post-war history. From research in local records they found that in 1946 the German government, through the industrial management company Industrieverwaltungsgesellschaft (IVG), leased buildings to mechanical, pharmaceutical and materials companies. Then, in 1966, land and buildings were systematically sold by IVG for the government to businesses and individuals. This was considered a great opportunity as the prices were cheap, the infrastructure good and at that time hardly anyone was concerned that the area was heavily contaminated by toxins left over from the manufacture of explosives.

By Project Week in 1983, Hirschhagen was the largest industrial area in the city of Hessisch Lichtenau and its largest employer with 600 jobs. At that time, some 200 people resided in Hirschhagen, many ex-refugees and their descendants who had been living in old leased bunkers and buildings for 30 years.

Some were families with children; about 30 children were living among the rubble in Hirschhagen. About half were toddlers and the rest school-age children who attended school in Hessisch Lichtenau. For the most part they were poor and lived in old buildings and bunkers that had interiors that had been renovated to make them habitable but outwardly they had hardly changed since the war. Only a few of the homes had been renovated both inside and out and these looked like welcoming bungalows.

In addition there were people living in Hirschhagen who could be characterized as adventurers, people who built a life in the blown-up areas, patching together homes from the wreckage and debris. These people found the chaotic terrain special and spooky, and liked the seclusion in this thickly-forested area.

In sharp contrast there was a group of more well-to-do people who lived on the premises of the small to medium-sized industrial companies where they worked.

Dieter Vaupel and his students devised a research plan for Project Week. For the demolished and dismantled buildings and bunkers they would employ the methods of archaeology and look for visible or hidden traces, document and try to decipher what exactly the Nazis had been doing there. Their plan was to let the ruins tell the story. They would also talk to as many of the people who lived there as they could to find out what they knew about the history of Hirschhagen.

Dieter recognized the project was monumental in scope – so many buildings and ruins to survey, so many people to talk to. He was not quite certain how much they could get done in only one week. Then, just before Project Week, one of the students came in with a truly astounding document that belonged to a member of his family – a 1949 map of the Hirschhagen area detailing a massive explosives factory with almost 400 buildings and a railway.

The map gave the project new impetus and level of excitement. No longer would the students be blindly exploring as they now knew what had been there, and exactly where it had been. Nothing could stop them from unearthing the truth.

3

An Adventure Playground

Not unlike the young Dieter Vaupel who played among the bombed out ruins and hidden tunnels of Spangenberg Castle, a number of the boys in the Project Week group had explored the demolished and decaying relics in the dense forest of Hirschhagen many times before; it was their adventure playground and they knew its ruins quite well.

Dieter was not surprised by the boys' fascination with the place. Hirschhagen was captivating in a Mad Max dystopian way, especially for teenage boys. Hirschhagen sneaks up on a person with its mysterious half-demolished buildings and ashen moonscapes seeming to appear in the forest out of nowhere. These relics could easily stretch the imagination – is this Shangri-la with an ethereal reflecting pool?

Figure 3: Building #313, the Denitrierung or Denitrification Building. Photo by Christel Bukowski.

The students would learn that this abandoned building was not something dreams were made of, but instead building #313 on their new-found map, the Denitrierung or Denitrification Building. Denitrification was used to reprocess the nitric and sulfuric acids from the factory, with the waste collected in the outdoor basin. When production in Hirschhagen was still running at full speed this water was so caustic that any person or animal that ventured in could not be expected to survive.

The dog whose demise in 1963 first alerted authorities that something was very wrong in Hirschhagen, had fallen into another pool just north of the Dentrification Building. By the time of Project Week in 1983, rainwater had diluted the malodorous liquid in this basin. Presumably, however, there were still remnants of the toxic substances in the previously emptied tanks. Most of these pools were already emptied in 1982 and the last one in 1984.

Another student favourite were the decaying concrete structures along the abandoned 35 kilometers of rail tracks that ran all through Hirschhagen. Dieter could understand their allure; resembling landing and take-off stations for alien spaceships, for the students it must have felt like being in a Star Wars movie. Their map revealed the more mundane purposes: these

Figure 4: Building #379, the Verladerampe or Loading Ramp. Photo by Christel Bukowski.

Figure 5: Skeleton of the Boiler House. Photo by Dieter Vaupel.

were ramps where armaments were loaded into railroad cars for transportation to the battlefronts.

Also compelling for young explorers was what their map revealed to be the skeleton of the acid boiler house. Here large cast-iron nitriding kettles once hung that were used to produce the highly toxic and explosive picric acid.

Those who played in and around the Boiler House did not know the area was highly contaminated. Authorities knew but this would not become public until the middle of the 1980s. The area where the Boiler House and also the other buildings in which toxic substances were cooked was renovated in the 1990s.

Many other contaminated sections were popular with young people, most notably the white-washed moonscapes that dotted the Hirschhagen forest. These Schleifschlammhalde or grinding sludge heaps were where combustible waste had been burned until the end of the war, and other production residues were stored. After the war, these heaps were covered with mud and other industrial wastes such as the slurry from the production of artificial marble.

✳✳✳

Dieter Vaupel could understand why his students were captivated by such monumental ruins and landscapes. Harder to grasp was their attraction to another type of playground on the Hirschhagen site. In the western area of Hirschhagen, away from the industrial area, was Relax Discotheque, a club where young people socialized and danced.

Housed in one of the Fertigungsgebäude or prefabricated buildings found throughout Hirschhagen, the particular building used by Relax had been assigned to the Pressengebäude or press building group. In the press buildings, igniters were produced or pressed in aluminum capsules. The primers were then removed, checked and packaged for later assembly with the explosives produced elsewhere on the site. Most of the prefabricated buildings had fallen into disrepair. The building used for Relax had been renovated with the addition of a new gable roof, and stood out among its rundown surroundings.

By 1983, Relax Discotheque had been in operation for a couple of years. Many of Dieter Vaupel's students, both boys and girls, went to Relax on a regular basis. For young people from Hessisch Lichtenau nothing could be more normal. What surprised Dieter was that no one cared about what had once gone on there.

This would change over the course of Project Week.

4

Field Trip

On the first day of Project Week Dieter Vaupel and his students were excited to tour Hirschhagen. While they had yet to find any written records of the factory in the Hessisch Lichtenau city archive or to interview any witnesses, they were still ready to uncover its history. They knew from the map that the area had been a munitions factory and they had a general sense of what the buildings had been used for. Their plan had two goals for the first day: do an initial exploration for an overview, and talk to some of the people living and working there.

The young people were also excited about a chance to explore some of the blown-up buildings, and their teacher Dieter Vaupel promised them a closer look. They would tour the site by foot, covering almost 10 kilometers and about a third of the 250-hectare site.

Their field trip began at the entrance to Hirschhagen, by the current administrative building originally used by the Nazis, and then straight past the old guard house.

Little did Dieter and the students suspect that they were about to tour what was not only the site of the largest munitions factories of the Deutsche Reich, but in fact one of the largest munitions factories in all of Europe during the Second World War. They did not know, for example, that construction of the factory began in 1936. They did not know that operations began in June 1938. And it never occurred to this group of students and their teacher from the local comprehensive school that they would be responsible for tearing from oblivion one of the darkest hidden chapters of Germany history.

First stop, they examined one of the loading buildings. Dieter and the students were right to surmise that here weapons were loaded and transported by train to the theatres of war. Near this loading building was one of the abandoned railroad cars that were common on the site. The group wondered not only *what* was transported to and from here, but *who* may have been transported in this railroad car to work here. The German people were already aware that slave labour had been part of the war effort. What the students had not known was how close it had been to their own homes, and what the people of Hessisch Lichtenau knew.

Next stop was in the redeveloped industrial area, the location marked on the map as Füllstation Ost or Filling Station East. This building was part of the complex where the bombs, grenades and mines were filled with TNT. Further research would reveal that Filling Station East had been the centre of production in the factory, the place most dangerous and harmful to health on the entire site. They also discovered that its counterpart, Filling Station West, had exploded during the war killing more than 70 people.

When the students reached Filling Station West they were surprised to discover it now housed a mundane manufacturer of metal appliances, a company that made fans.

From the commercial industrial area Dieter and the students ventured into the forest, passing fenced-off areas where entrance was forbidden. They encountered a variety of pipes and metal structures in the forest. There were large steel stands that had supported the above-ground pipes in which liquid intermediate and end-products were pumped from one building to another.

Figure 6: Students, map in hand, walk past #567, Toilet House. Photo by Dieter Vaupel.

Some of the pipes still held fragments of heavy insulation; the pipes were insulated and heated because the liquids had to be at a controlled temperature. The students' initial guess about the exposed pipes proved correct: the lines were laid above ground so that in the event of an explosion the damage could be immediately seen and the lines quickly repaired to maintain production.

As they trekked through the forest they came upon an abandoned structure the map revealed to be building #576 on their map, an old toilet house.

They soon found what appeared to be another abandoned toilet house. Closer examination showed that someone was actually converting it into a home, but there was no one there at the time.

In the forest they passed a number of former bunkers that had also been renovated into homes. Bunkers were buildings that served as, for example, storage for the blanks where preparatory work was done, warehouses for different materials used in the production process or packing houses. Some bunkers had been so thoroughly remodelled that their former purpose could not be recognized.

Dieter and the students wondered how people could live in these buildings if they had known their history, and especially now knowing there was poison in the ground and the water. Perhaps, they thought, it was a matter of price. The buildings must have been almost free for the taking, at the cost of renovation.

The group had hoped to interview residents during their field trip but discovered that no one would talk to them. Dieter was not surprised considering many lived in very secluded areas, some of them for 30 years. Over the coming years, however, most of the residents of Hirschhagen would closely follow Dieter's investigation, and would be very critical of his work. This would not change until another generation arrived who were more open to the realities of Hirschhagen.

About 40 press buildings stood in different parts of the factory, in two groups in the eastern and western sections. The most well-known to the students now housed the Relax Discotheque. Dieter and the group decided to closely examine one of the abandoned press buildings in the western part that was freely accessible, Building #367.

Dieter and the students entered the Press Building. He asked them how they could learn something about the work that used to be done there. They already had one clue as 'Press Building' was shown on the map as the functional name of the building.

The students were trying to reconstruct the floor plan when next to an opening in the wall they discovered the following inscription: 'Note the press

Figure 7: Students in Press Building #367, Hirschhagen. Photo by Dieter Vaupel.

operator! Before pressing, light signal and barrier! During pressing, pointer and manometer! After pressing, quality and dimensions of the body!'

This gave the students some further insight into what had been done in the building. Other traces were discovered: connections for machines, a pipeline network and finally another inscription next to a water pipe: 'Harmful! No drinking water' including the same text in French. This was the first indication that Germans had not been the only workers here.

Dieter and the students left Hirschhagen that first day satisfied that their visit was productive. For the next day, Dieter had found someone who had been a resistance fighter imprisoned by the Nazis in Buchenwald concentration camp. This man had some information about Hirschhagen during the war and was willing to come to Hessisch Lichtenau to talk to the students. What he would say would leave them speechless.

5

First Witness

Dieter Vaupel first heard about Max Mayr from a teaching colleague who had read about the 86-year-old in a newspaper in Kassel, where they both lived. A former political prisoner tortured by the Gestapo for his anti-Nazi views, in 1936 Max was tried and sentenced to prison, then eventually sent to Buchenwald concentration camp. As Max had been speaking at schools, Dieter thought he could bring a welcome first-hand perspective to his students – even though Dieter had no idea what Max knew about what had happened in Hessisch Lichtenau.

The Project Week student group was composed of six girls and nine boys, who were mostly upper secondary school pupils between the ages of 17 and 18 years old, with a few 15 and 16 year-olds still in intermediate school. After the field trip to Hirschhagen, Dieter had a better understanding of how much they knew and how they felt about Germany under the Nazis. At best, they had a fragmentary understanding of their area's history during that time.

Dieter had also learned something about why the students joined this particular group, reasons which differed sharply between the boys and girls. For the boys it seemed the topic was interesting not only because many of them had grown up exploring and playing on the factory site in Hirschhagen, but also because talking about it was strongly taboo. At the time, people in Germany knew that terrible things had happened in places such as Auschwitz during National Socialism, and this had been dealt with in politics, school and society. But what had happened on their own doorstep, and the fact that it happened only because many took part, was something that most Germans would just as soon prefer remain unspoken and buried in the past.

Some of the boys who had already explored Hirschhagen had also heard one or two mysterious stories about the site. There were stories of bodies flying into the air and a place called the chocolate factory. They wanted to know more.

For the girls, their primary interest was decidedly different. Like the boys, they had been taught about the Nazi era in Germany in the classroom, and like the boys they had learned that speaking about it at home was impossible as their parents did not want to talk about it. However, the girls as a group had a very specific motivation: they wanted to know whether the people of Hessisch Lichtenau knew about or took part in the horrors of the Nazi regime.

Whatever their reasons for taking part in the Project Week group, Dieter soon became aware that all of the students felt a tension from home for working on the topic. Yet only one boy had parents who forced him to drop out. All the rest remained.

***

Max Mayr came to visit the students at the Freiherr-vom-Stein-Schule in Hessisch Lichtenau on the second day of Project Week. Max was from Kassel, a city about 30 kilometers from Hessisch Lichtenau. Kassel was the district capital of North Hesse as well as the capital of the government-sponsored tourist initiative, the Fairy Tale Route. Kassel was where the Brothers Grimm lived and worked, collecting and transcribing the tales of Cinderella, Sleeping Beauty, Snow White, Little Red Riding Hood and many others.

Kassel was also known as a city that had been severely impacted by the Second World War. Home to major aircraft, heavy tank, locomotive and engine plants, Kassel was a major target of Allied strategic bombing attacks, with one so severe that part of the city burned for seven days, killing 10,000 people. Kassel's population of 236,000 in 1939 had diminished to 50,000 by the end of the war.

What first impressed Dieter about Max Mayr was how the 86-year-old, even though frail, still had a commanding presence and a solid grasp of the facts he was reporting. The students and Dieter were in rapt attention the entire time he spoke.

The son of a weaver who trained as a machinist, Max was inducted and served as a soldier in the First World War. He returned home in 1918 a bitter opponent of war and joined the Communist Party (KPD) and later the International Socialist Alliance (ISK). After returning from war, he worked at the Henschel company in Kassel as a lathe operator, until moving to Berlin to serve as editor for a socialist magazine from 1932-1933.

After the Nazis came to power, Max returned to Kassel and the Henschel company, working in armaments production by day and with an illegal political resistance group by night. Unfortunately for Max, the resistance group was betrayed by a Gestapo agent. Max was tortured, tried by a court in Kassel and sentenced to two and a half years at a facility in Kassel Wehlheiden. In 1938 he was sent to the Buchenwald concentration camp where prisoners were put to work. After two years he managed to get assigned to the camp clerk office where he would remain until the camp was

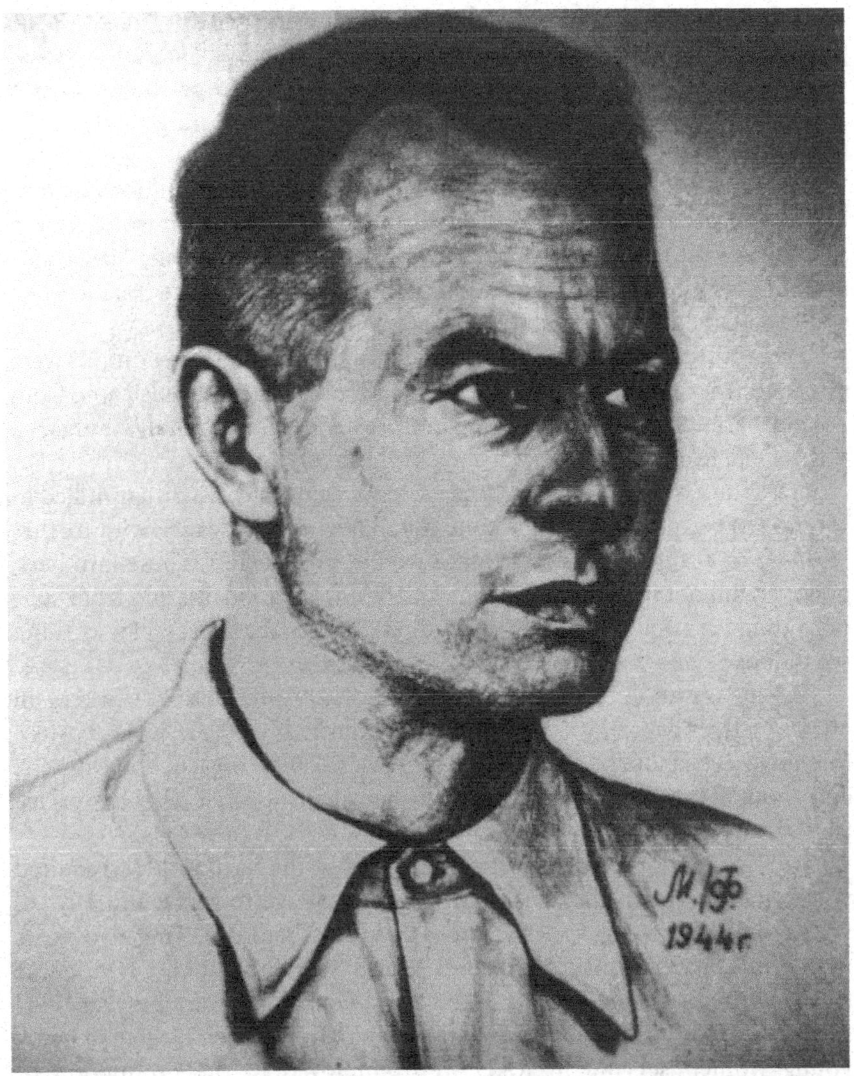

Figure 8 Max Mayr at Buchenwald, as drawn by a fellow prisoner. Private photo from Max Mayr published in Jörg Kammler und Dietfried Krause Vilmar (Herausgeber/ Editor): *Volksgemeinschaftund Volksfeinde. Kassel 1933-1945* (Kassel: Hesse GmbH 1984), p.363.

liberated in 1945. During his time at Buchenwald, Max was also part of the illegal camp resistance.

Max told the students that working as a commandant clerk provided opportunities to aid his fellow prisoners. 'I was able to help the camp inmates through this work, that their appeal was made as quickly as possible, that everything was right. I could also help many through my position by providing them with a better work assignment where the labour statistics showed they would be a little less stressed. Or I could get them off bad transports or get them something extra to eat by assigning work in the kitchen.'

Then Max talked about Hessisch Lichtenau and the munitions factory in Hirschhagen. He told the students he had this information from his role at Buchenwald, and also from the work he did after the war. Max was a founding member of the Association of the Prosecutors of the Nazi Regime and had worked for the Kassel reparation authority.

He recalled that thousands of people from many different countries were forced to work in the munitions factory in Hirschhagen. People came from Poland, France, Netherlands, Belgium, Soviet Union, Italy, Bulgaria, Yugoslavia, Romania, Spain, Czechoslovakia and Hungary.

It was an extremely dangerous place to work, he said, with many killed in several large explosions. At the time Max knew of 150 deaths; with further research in ensuing years this figure would grow to 180. These numbers, however, did not include the victims killed in work accidents and from slow poisoning, as well as people who died due to the miserable working conditions.

By the summer of 1944, there were 4,400 production workers in Hirschhagen, including 2,300 women. About half of these workers were foreign forced labourers. In addition there were 2,000 construction workers, and about 800 members of the Reichsarbeitsdienst or Reich Labor Service (RAD).

RAD, the national work service established by the Nazis in 1934, required young men between the ages of 18-25 years of age to serve. Initially, all young men had to go to RAD for six months before serving two years in the military. During the Second World War their RAD service was shortened as they were needed in the army. During the war one-year RAD service became compulsory for young women. In Hessisch Lichtenau many young women serving in RAD were employed in the production of explosives.

In August 1944 the total number of workers at the site would jump to more than 8,000 when 1,000 Hungarian Jewish women and girls were sent from Auschwitz concentration camp to work the most dangerous jobs in the munitions factory in Hirschhagen.

When Max spoke about the Jewish women and girls sent to Hessisch Lichtenau from Auschwitz, Dieter could see the disbelief on the students' faces. Perhaps Max saw it too but he continued unfazed. He finished his narrative and asked if the students had any questions.

How did he know there were concentration camp inmates sent to Hessisch Lichtenau? Max explained that in his role as a commandant clerk, he had first-hand knowledge of the Hungarian Jewish women being sent from Auschwitz, as the labour camp in Hessisch Lichtenau was a Buchenwald outpost.

Max shuffled through the papers he had brought with him. He held up a list with Außenkommandos or 'female external details' for the Buchenwald concentration camp from 25 November 1944. Außenkommandos was the term used to describe a basic unit or detachment of slave labourers in concentration camps.

There were 136 Außenkommandos sent out from Buchenwald. One of them, to Hessisch Lichtenau, had 1,003 women named as 'additions' and the 'actual strength' listed as 792 women.

Max explained why there was such a discrepancy between the number of women and girls sent from Auschwitz deemed 'additions' as opposed to 'actual strength'. He could account for 206 of the women.

After three months the commandant of their labour camp asked who among them needed a lighter work load because of their physical condition or if they were pregnant. A number of the women and girls raised their hands. These volunteers, along with those in the sick bay, a total of 206 women and girls, were put on cattle cars and sent back to Auschwitz. Upon arrival they were immediately gassed.

When the Jewish women and girls first arrived from Auschwitz they were housed in Lager Vereinshaus, a camp located on the outskirts of the city of Hessisch Lichtenau between Hopfelder Strasse and Heinrich Strasse. Originally built for 700 construction workers, part of Lager Vereinshaus was partitioned off and fenced with barbed wire to accommodate the women. There were many other camps grouped around the factory to house workers, and Max recited their names: Friedrichsbrück camp, Herzog camp, Lenoir camp, Teichhof camp, Föhren camp, Esche camp and Steinbach camp. Some had permanent fixed buildings, some were makeshift barracks or tents, and each had its own specific population.

Camp Waldhof had fixed buildings for up to 1,500 persons. Initially it housed only German female employees, but later also held French female slave workers.

Camp Herzog had fixed buildings for up to 1,200 persons, that until 1942 held only German workers, and then mainly Dutch and French. The fixed buildings of Camp Lenoirstift housed only German female workers.

Camp Teichhof held wooden barracks that housed 1,000 German employees and RAD workers.

Camp Friedrichsbrück was a makeshift camp for up to 350 construction workers.

Figure 9: German workers, Camp Waldhof, 1943. Private Archive Dieter Vaupel.

The barracks of Camp Föhren were inhabited by German workers in 1939 and later by foreign workers. From 1943, 300-400 forced labourers from Ukraine, some 10 to 12 year-old girls, lived there.

Camp Esche und Steinbach's wooden barracks could hold up to 1,000 persons. Initially these were construction workers, and later women and girls from the Ukraine and Soviet prisoners of war.

Max Mayr did not have any photos of the worker camps to show the students, but in his later research Dieter Vaupel eventually found design drawings of the barracks from the Hessisch Lichtenau City Archives.

After the war the barracks were rented out for different purposes. A barrack in Lager Vereinshaus that housed the women and girls from Auschwitz became a butcher shop selling horsemeat.

Did the local people of Hessisch Lichtenau know that women and girls from Auschwitz were working in the factory? Of course they did, Max maintained. To get to and from the explosives factory or the train station, the women were marched through Hessisch Lichtenau, past townspeople and houses. Additionally, many of the villagers worked in the factory or in the camps.

Of course everybody knew.

At that point, Max Mayr was met with a stunned silence. The class had no more questions. Dieter Vaupel thanked him for coming, and he left the now quiet classroom.

***

Not long after Max Mayr's classroom appearance, one of the boys in the Project Week group came in with a map of the camps where the workers were housed that he said a friend had given to him.

6

Chocolate Factory

Encouraged by the testimony of Max Mayr, students in the Project Week group approached family, friends and neighbours in Hessisch Lichtenau about what they might know about the factory and the slave workers. The students quickly secured interviews from two brave Hessisch Lichtenau residents willing to break the taboo and talk about the Nazi era, Heinrich Kleinschmidt and Berta Schröder. Six more townspeople were willing to be interviewed anonymously.

Heinrich Kleinschmidt was already known to many of the students, as he lived directly opposite the Freiherr-vom-Stein-Schule where he also ran an electric shop and a small bike shop. He agreed to visit the classroom to tell his story and provide a written account. He was glad his town was finally confronting what had happened there.

An electrician by trade, Heinrich's military service was cut short so he could work in the German shipbuilding centres of Kiel and then Rostock, and finally in Lithuania. Whenever he was allowed time off from this work he would visit his family in Hessisch Lichtenau, ask his wife and children what was going on in the town and observe the activities himself.

Heinrich told the students that the first buildings of the munitions factory were built in 1936 in the area called Hirschhagen today. At that time it belonged to the Lichtenau district of Fürstenhagen and was a pristine mixed forest area. More land was also expropriated to build airfields; locals watched as the potatoes in the fields were not harvested and left to rot.

During this time, the townspeople were required to watch government films shown at the local Green Tree Inn. To Heinrich these propaganda films were part of Hitler's effort to dumb down the people and make them more compliant.

In the early days of the factory, the workers were Germans from the region; there was high unemployment and people were happy to finally have a job again. When these workers were no longer sufficient for the expanding factory, additional German workers were recruited from outside the area. Once the war started, foreign workers were first drawn from the occupied countries, first Poland, later especially France and The Netherlands, by promises of good wages, mail every four weeks and a vacation every six months.

In 1941, 201 Italians were employed at Hessisch Lichtenau under a contract with Mussolini. When there were no more volunteers, the so-called 'subhumans' were gathered and brought to Germany by force in trucks. These included the Poles and Soviets brought to Hessisch Lichtenau as forced labourers after the invasions of their countries.

Heinrich recalled that the Poles wore a 'P' on their clothing, and some were housed in a former cigar factory confiscated from a Jewish businessman, Mr Wolff. The city of Hessisch Lichtenau had appropriated the cigar factory as part of 'Aryanization', then leased it to the construction company Röder & Küllmer who housed construction workers there, including Poles. This was not one of the camps Max Mayr had listed in his presentation, and unlike many of the other camps it was right in the town and not in the countryside.

The Polish workers were allowed to leave their camp and go into town. Among them was a 15-year-old boy who would gather trash for pigs or chop wood for townspeople, including Heinrich's family, in exchange for soap and razors. But the rules were clear – if a Pole dared to try and buy cigarettes in the Green Tree Inn, or some other such audacious act, the local police would beat them. In Heinrich's eyes it seemed that every policeman wanted to stand out and be more sadistic than the SA or SS.

Eventually more and more workers were needed in the explosives factory, Heinrich told the students. At the same time, following the defeat of the German army in Stalingrad in 1943, the flow of prisoners of war and forced labourers who could be deported to Germany decreased dramatically. For this reason Jews were allowed to stay alive, especially women aged 15 to 40 who were healthy and strong.

When the war reached its final stage, Hitler was desperately trying to produce more munitions by any and all means. In 1944, 1,000 Jewish women and girls were brought in from Auschwitz to Lager Vereinshaus in Hessisch Lichtenau.

As Heinrich Kleinschmidt spoke of Jewish women and girls being held in their town, Dieter Vaupel and his students recognized the significance of the moment: he had corroborated a major revelation made by Max Mayr.

Lager Vereinshaus was named after an adjacent building on Heinrichstrasse where various associations held activities – 'Verein' is the German word for association – and where a kindergarten and school were once housed. The camp consisted of 10 barracks, each 10 by 30 meters in size, and auxiliary buildings such as toilets, showers, a building for the guards and a warehouse. The barracks stood on the site of a former nursery bordered by Heinrichstrasse and Hopfelder Strasse.

Figure 10: Posing for a photo on Heinrichstrasse behind Lager Vereinshaus barracks, 1943. Private Archive Dieter Vaupel.

Lager Vereinshaus, located in the city of Hessisch Lichtenau, stood five kilometers from the munitions factory. Each day the emaciated Jewish labourers were force-marched through the town's streets to their work.

The factory, Heinrich explained, was popularly known as the 'chocolate factory' as people were afraid to express its actual purpose. The Hessisch Lichtenau factory was operated by a subsidiary of Dynamit Nobel AG with the official description given as 'limited liability company for the recycling of chemical products' or 'recycling chemistry' (Verwertchemie) for short. Some residents of Hessisch Lichtenau called the plant 'muna', a trivialization of the term munitions factory (Munitionsfabrik).

✱✱✱

In 2020, in preparation for this book, Dieter Vaupel spoke to Heinrich Kleinschmidt's son Hubert. Born in 1935, Hubert was nine years old when the Jewish women were brought to Hessisch Lichtenau. At that time the family lived on Kirchstrasse, very close to the camp. He saw the women marching past their house every day when they went to the factory. They were pitifully dressed, had shaved heads and in the winter they wrapped newspaper around their legs against the cold. He said he still has pictures of them in his mind today.

In those days, Hubert told Dieter, there was a bakery near the Kleinschmidt house. Every morning, like work horses, the Jewish girls would pull a cart to the bakery. Under the watchful eyes of the SS guards the cart was loaded with bread and the team of girls would haul it back to the camp.

Hubert recalled seeing a Jewish girl up close in the waiting room of the doctor. An SS man brought her there, as she had badly injured her hand in an accident at work. The young Hubert was impressed that the doctor was very professional, treating her immediately before all the other patients. However, the doctor also scolded her for being so careless. Hubert did not understand the doctor's reaction; certainly she did not intentionally injure herself so badly. As a boy he remembered thinking she must certainly be driven to work so hard.

After the war Hubert's father Heinrich Kleinschmidt operated his electrical business and bicycle shop in part of a barrack of the Vereinshaus camp. This barrack was jointly occupied by an ironmongery and a textile business. The barrack was bought by Heinrich in 1948, dismantled in the camp and installed on Leipziger Strasse in Hessisch Lichtenau.

Years later the Kleinschmidt family would build a new house on Freiherr-vom-Stein-Strasse. They would live here and run their business right across the street from the school where Heinrich Kleinschmidt would one day come and talk to Dieter Vaupel and his students about what had happened in their town.

✳✳✳

Berta Schröder had lived in Hessisch Lichtenau all her life. Dieter and a few students went to the elderly woman's home after she agreed to be interviewed for Project Week. They found her to be very empathetic, and still haunted by the suffering of the Jews.

Berta was among the townspeople who began working in the munitions factory when it first started production in 1938. She told the students that she eventually became a foreman overseeing the work of mainly Poles and Russians, but also some Italians. When the Jewish women first arrived at the train station in Hessisch Lichtenau in 1944, Berta recalled being at home on a lunch break. Someone came and told her there was a train with lots of freight cars with Jews inside. In her interview Berta described how she watched the Jews pass her house in a column on their way to Lager Vereinshaus:

They were only women, young women, although it was difficult to tell their age. One looked much like the other, everyone was emaciated, had shaved heads and wore sack clothes. I cannot say how many there were, but certainly well over a hundred. Women and older men guarded them. A man carried a bucket of water to refresh those who were exhausted from the train ride. There were some (townspeople) who laughed and scoffed at the sad column of people. Most ignored them.

The Jewish women and girls were assigned to the most dangerous job at the factory: the filling stations. According to Berta:

They [the Jewish women] had to work with acid, which made them sick. Their faces, hands and arms were yellow or even green, and the hair turned red. Some looked grass green! When the Jews were sick, they were simply put back on trains like cattle and shipped back to the concentration camp. There were often accidents in the filling stations. The bunkers were built in such a way that the walls and people were thrown out in the event of an explosion, but the concrete scaffolding remained standing. I remember several large explosions. People's bodies were totally torn apart and bones and clothing hung in the trees. The people from Lichtenau did not pay much attention to the Jews.

In 1984 Dieter Vaupel would visit Berta Schröder to thank her for being one of the first residents of Hessisch Lichtenau to openly talk about what happened there and to give her a copy of his new book on the camp. A local newspaper, the *Hessisch Niedersächsische Allgemeine*, covered this visit.

In addition to Heinrich Kleinschmidt and Berta Schröder, on the promise of anonymity Dieter and the students interviewed six townspeople who either worked in the factory and/or lived near Lager Vereinshaus.

***

Mr E. started working in the explosives factory in 1938, in a section where plate mines, designed to damage tanks, were filled with explosives. He recalled the work was done in three 8-hours shifts – and that there were numerous explosions. Building 305 exploded for the first time on 6 September 1938. Two men from town were killed: Heinrich Möller and Moritz Gossmann. In 1940 an explosion in the filling station caused numerous injuries and severe burns. There was a second explosion in the filling station in 1943, when 40 people, mostly Russian girls, were killed. Only fragments remained from the bodies of these girls. In 1944 a filling station exploded again, and there was a death. (Today we know there was a large explosion on 31 March 1944, in which the entire Filling Station West building complex was destroyed and a total of 73 people died: 18 Soviets, 17 Germans, 17 Italians, 9 Dutch, 7 French, 4 Poles and 1 Bulgarian.)

***

Mrs B. worked in the factory laboratory and lived on Hopfelder Strasse next to the Lager Vereinshaus. Shortly before the Jews came in 1944, she saw a chain-link fence with barbed wire on top installed around the camp. There was also a watchtower and a few guardhouses. Older men from Hessisch Lichtenau were responsible for outside security and surveillance. These men Mrs B. characterized as 'stupid geese'. Most of the Jewish women were under 40 and emaciated. Mrs B's mother often bribed the old men working as security guards so she could throw some bread over the fence for the Jews to eat.

Mrs B. also remembered the Jewish women having shaved heads and yellow skin from handling chemicals. In winter they wrapped rags or newspapers around their legs. Some walked to work barefoot and some had Dutch wooden shoes. SS women would beat them on the legs with sticks and whips.

The Lichtenau population took no notice of the Jewish women but in the factory, some townspeople, at risk of their own lives, would hand a loaf of bread to the Jewish women as they passed.

In the last days before the camp was cleared, some Jews made it over the fence and fled towards Reichenbach. They ran to the forest and were never found.

After the camp was cleared Mrs B. had to scrub the barracks. It was infested with insects. The Jewish women slept on wooden beds without mattresses.

***

During the last years of the war Mrs F. taught students in the Auguste-Viktoria-Haus, a primary school right next door to Lager Vereinshaus. Mrs F. remembered:

> When we were outside with the students, the Jews came to the fence and begged. They looked miserable and had yellow skin. Their clothes consisted of sack cloths tied together in the middle with a rope. I still remember the harrowing sight when I went to school in the morning

and had to walk past the camp. The Jews were guarded, but they could get to the fence. There were always women in the camp because they worked in shifts in the factory. Once I accidentally got into the Jewish special car that was coupled to our train. At first, I looked at the women somewhat astonished. One of them said in broken German: 'We don't do anything!' I sat down in the open space and, as I did not want to make the Jewess uncomfortable, I read a book. A young woman who sat across from me said: 'Oh, I once have a book just like this one!'

***

Mrs A. lived next to Lager Vereinshaus on Hopfelder Strasse. She found that some of the guards patrolling the fence around the camp would let her throw food to the miserable looking and hungry Jews if she bribed them with cake.

On Saturdays I baked cakes for the women, packed them in shoe boxes, tied them up and threw them over the fence. I had bribed the guards with cake beforehand. We sometimes called out to each other over the fence when there were no guards around. Women who could speak German said: 'We don't reject anything!' One said: 'I have three blond boys, who knows what is with them. Maybe they are already dead.' I tried to comfort the women.

Mrs A. would go to the fence and throw something over: clothes, shoes and especially something to eat, mostly when it was dark. 'I had to be careful because the guards were constantly patrolling the fence. Some men were reasonable, but there was one who even threatened to shoot me. I wouldn't be the first, he said.'

Many times Mrs A would see the Jewish women and girls being led out of the camp gate on Heinrichstrasse and ordered to sing a song. SS who were in front, behind and on the sides, drove the Jews with whips, slapped them on their feet and shouted: 'Go, Ios!'

In the days before evacuation, some Jews fled the camp by digging a hole under the fences and fleeing into the forest. The guards found out and searched for them for some time but could not find them. After the war a Jewish woman came to Mrs A. with a Pole and accused her of betraying the Jewish prisoners. 'But I would never have done that. I knew how the women were doing.'

***

Mr D's father was a master craftsman whose family lived in the settlement in Fürstenhagen, a village two and a half kilometers from Hessisch Lichtenau. The explosives factory was built in a large forest area that belonged to the village of Fürstenhagen. After the Second World War this area where the explosives factory was built became a separate district of Hessisch Lichtenau and was named Hirschhagen.

Mr D. told the student interviewers:

> I was still a child, but I still remember some of the events from that time. From the Fürstenhagen station a footpath that was about 1.50 meters wide led up towards the Munitlonsfabrik. I stood one day in the summer of 1944 as an 11-year-old boy on this path when around 100 Jewish women were brought up there. The Jews came up the path. They were slim young women with shaved heads. They had uniform suits. Today I would say that you could see from the outside that they had been specially selected to carry out hard and dangerous work.

Mr D. recognized one of security guards. The man was from Rommerode, a small village about five kilometers from Hessisch Lichtenau, a butcher who had slaughtered in Mr D's house. He spoke to the guard but was told not to speak to him or the women. Mr D. could not understand this but realized something was not right. The sight of the woman stayed with him.

> I can still see the women as they come up the path in front of me today. They came every day with a special train from Hessisch Lichtenau, a locomotive with converted freight cars. When you saw the Jews as they came up the path, you could see that despite everything, they had not lost their pride.

***

From August 1944 to March 1945, Mrs C. worked for the armaments office as a controller for the filling station. Of all the witnesses she had the most contact with the Jewish women and girls.

> Hungarian Jews from the Vereinshaus camp worked with us every day at the filling station and we did the same work. There was a very good, almost friendly relationship between us and the Jews. We had always been told that the Jews were subhumans and now there were Jewish

girls from Hungary who should work with us. It was so amazing and unbelievable for us, because these cheerful and exuberant girls did not really correspond to the picture that had always been conveyed to us. Most of them were very young and despite their shaved hair there were many pretty girls among them. Little by little we learned a something about the fate of the girls and we all felt sorry for them.

A teacher, called Maria, who was about 40 years old, was our interpreter. This woman did not work on the line like other Jews in the filling station, but was a kind of supervisor for the girls. She was actually older than the girls. The girls were all very young, probably my age, about 20 years. Maria and others have told how they were deported to Auschwitz, where they all had to undress and how all their clothes and private belongings were taken off. They got new clothes, wooden clogs and baggy clothes…

I can still clearly remember Christmas 1944. I had a late shift on Christmas Eve. It was work around the clock, including weekends and public holidays. After the late shift, we had a Christmas party in the filling area, the Jewish women also celebrated. A local man had brought a Christmas tree with him. We were happy and exuberant that evening and sang. The Jews even sang our German Christmas carols. But they also sang and danced Hungarian songs…

There were many intelligent girls among the Jews, including a whole lot of students. One could draw well. She made a portrait of me. Unfortunately I don't have it anymore…

One day the caretaker Maria told us that one of the girls was pregnant and asked if we knew of anyone who could provide an abortion. There was a nurse who did this, but she was in prison because she was caught. So we could not help the girl. A short time later I brought her a body bandage from my mother. I remember that despite her condition, the girl had sung and danced with us at Christmas. She still had three sisters. They looked confusingly similar. At the beginning of the next year, the girl no longer showed up. I do not know what happened to her…

Mrs C. could not speak first-hand to the girls' life in the camp. She only knew what the girls told her, such as washing clothing on Saturdays and having to wrap themselves in blankets as they had nothing else to wear. With her husband she would sometimes go for a walk in town around the camp. The Jews generally had no curtains so you could see them. Anyone who walked by could see them.

Mrs C. said she was glad that Dieter Vaupel and his students were asking about the Jewish women and girls; the younger people of Hessisch Lichtenau should know.

***

After the war the barracks in Lager Vereinshaus were routinely used for other purposes. Heinrich Kleinschmidt's shop is one example. Another barrack was used as a cinema in Hessisch Lichtenau for many years. There were also barracks dismantled and taken out of Hessisch Lichtenau, such as the one rebuilt in the forest in Reichenbach, the same forest some Jewish women and girls had escaped to and were never found. This barrack would serve as a recreational camp for young people unaware of its history.

7

Open House

Before Project Week, Nazi war crimes had happened in places such as Auschwitz, the extermination camp in Poland, or Buchenwald, the concentration camp only 100 kilometers from Hessisch Lichtenau. This is what the students had learned in school, and many had seen first-hand when they visited Buchenwald's prison buildings, gallows and crematorium.

The students all knew that these dark places were where the Nazis had committed the crimes prosecuted after the war. Not in somewhere like Hessisch Lichtenau, their fairy-tale town where their own families lived. But then they heard what Max Mayr, Heinrich Kleinschmidt, Berta Schröder and six anonymous townspeople had to say.

Their town had been home to one of the largest munitions factory of the Deutsche Reich. The factory ran on the work of thousands of slave labourers. The labourers included nearly 1,000 Jewish women and girls sent from Auschwitz, who were barely fed, beaten by guards and slowly poisoned by the chemicals they were forced to handle. In a matter of days the image of their bucolic hometown had been turned on its head. They wanted answers. Who else knew what happened here?

The students were now driven to find out how many of their townsfolk shared this awareness. They wanted to *do* something. Dieter helped them to productively focus their outrage. They would go out on the streets of Hessisch Lichtenau and politely ask: 'What did you know about the Nazi era in Hessisch Lichtenau?'

One group, three or four students, stood on Poststrasse, a main thoroughfare in Hessisch Lichtenau with some shops and restaurants, where there were always people walking.

Another group went to Heinrichstrasse, in front of the former site of Lager Vereinshaus, the camp where the Jewish women and girls had been housed. The camp was long gone and in its place stood the newly-opened Freiherr-vom-Stein-Schule, a school for students ages 11 and 12 as well as a primary school.

The students at both locations, Poststrasse and Heinrichstrasse, tried to address passers-by but had no success. No one wanted to answer the question. People just kept on walking or said it was a long time ago and there was no reason for it to be discussed today. It was better to leave the past alone.

Some passers-by said that they knew nothing about it because they had not lived in Hessisch Lichtenau at the time. This was certainly true for some, as many people who had been displaced by the war or refugees from the former German territories in the east, ended up in Hessisch Lichtenau.

The students, of course, were disappointed by the lack of response.

***

Project Week ran from Monday-Friday with an Open House on Saturday. It was a major school event with more than 1,000 students who worked on over 50 different project topics presenting their results. The students in Dieter Vaupel's group worried they would not have enough documentation by Saturday's Open House to corroborate what Max Mayr, Heinrich Kleinschmidt, Berta Schröder and six townspeople had told them.

In their initial meetings before Project Week, students had contacted the town government and state agencies and archives for information on Hessisch Lichtenau during the Nazi era. The response from the Archives for the City of Hessisch Lichtenau was brief and dismissive: No documents were available about the Nazi era. They were all burned by the Mayor of Lichtenau shortly before the Americans marched in.

This turned out to be wrong. Only a few years later trained historians would unearth extensive material on the war years in the attic of the town hall. But for the Open House, the students had no records from the town.

The response from State Archives in Marburg was not a complete rebuff but was not much help for the Open House presentation. The State Archives had no documents, as far as they knew, but the students were welcome to visit the archives and do their own research.

Then, finally, the students received a positive response and the corroboration they needed. They were told in a letter from International Tracing Service (ITS) Bad Arolsen that the Vereinshaus camp in Hessisch Lichtenau accommodated up to 1,000 predominantly Hungarian Jews, who were assigned to Buchenwald concentration camp as an external command. At that time, however, the ITS Bad Arolsen, an archive on the victims of Nazi persecution, was not yet accessible for historical research by outside groups, so this short letter was all they had.

And then, a second corroboration arrived from the Hessian State Archive confirming that the Jewish women and girls had been there. The letter was also brief but had more detail:

Unfortunately, no documents relating to the ammunition works or the persecution of the Jews can be found in the archives of the Nazi era located here. It is only known that in Hessisch Lichtenau from August 1st, 1944 to March 29th 1945 there was an external command of the Buchenwald concentration camp, which consisted of about 800 women, mostly Hungarian Jews. As a result of work accidents, more than 150 deaths have occurred in the factory (= limited liability company for the use of chemical products).

With these letters, the students could now finish their preparations for Open House. Between their field trip to the site of the munitions factory in Hirschhagen, the interviews of Max Mayr, Heinrich Kleinschmidt, Berta Schröder and townspeople, and the letters confirming the Jewish women and girls had been sent from Auschwitz, they were confident in presenting their controversial findings.

***

The projects were presented either in classrooms or in the large break hall. Dieter and his students picked a central place in the break hall so as many visitors as possible would see their display. They filled two pin walls with posters that contained photos and documents. The students and Dieter stood by the display to answer questions and offer clarifications.

As usual, the visitors to the Open House were mostly parents. Of the over 1,000 who attended, about 100 showed interest in Dieter and the students' exhibition. Most were shocked at the suggestion that their town had held a major munitions factory, and slave workers from Auschwitz as well.

A few visitors said it was admirable that the students helped uncover a dark chapter in the city's history. But hardly anyone wanted to believe that there really was a concentration camp external command in Hessisch Lichtenau with 1,000 women who were delivered from Auschwitz. If there had been anything like that, some insisted, then they would have heard of it long ago. It would have been in the history books. A member of the school management went so far as to tell Dieter not to tell lies. This man was certain there was never a concentration camp in Hessisch Lichtenau.

There were also those who did not question whether it happened, but echoed what the students had heard on the street: why not leave the past alone?

It was clear to Dieter that they had managed to only scratch the surface when it came to the women and the factory. Encountering resistance in their research made Dieter want to find out more. Some of the students felt the same.

However, what was especially disturbing to the students at the Open House was the callousness of visitors as regards the Jewish women and girls. Very few of the visitors expressed any remorse or pity for them. In sharp contrast, many of the students had come to identify with the Jewish girls sent to Hessisch Lichtenau as they were the same age.

After the Open House the students wanted to know the fate of these women and girls who had come from Auschwitz to suffer in Hessisch Lichtenau. They did not want people to forget this. Dieter offered the students the chance to continue working on the project on a volunteer basis. They would meet once a week after school. The students who were not graduating welcomed the opportunity to participate.

In November 1983, the first major article about Dieter and the students researching the Jewish women and girls would appear in the local newspaper *Hessisch Niedersächsische Allgemeine* (HNA), 'A Thousand Jews in Lichetenau Camp'.

By our editor Werner Keller:

Hess. Lichtenau / Helsa. The relics of the darkest chapter in German history are in Hess. Lichtenau still to be found. In the Hirschhagen forest area, very close to Helsa's Waldhof settlement, there are dilapidated bunkers, remains of one of the largest explosives factories in the Third Reich. There are many dark memories surrounding Hirschhagen while Lichtenauer and Helsaer know more or less about it.

What is new is that it is on the outskirts of Hess. Lichtenau is said to have given a strong external command of the Buchenwald concentration camp, which included a camp with around a thousand female prisoners: Jewish women from Eastern European countries who were employed to work in the ammunition factory.

Book planned
The teacher Dieter Vaupel (34) from Spangenberg, who works at the comprehensive school in Hess, has now found clear evidence of this. Lichtenau is active. He has his findings in the writing 'The concentration camp external command Hess. Lichtenau 1944/45', which is part of a book on concentration camp sub-camps in Hesse. This book is due to be published by Eichborn-Verlag Frankfurt in January. The editor is Lothar Bembenek.

Project week

For teacher Vaupel, work started in the spring when a project week took place at the comprehensive school. One group went on the topic 'Hess. Lichtenau in the Nazi era'. One came across the Hirschhagen plant and the connection between Hess. Lichtenau and Buchenwald. From then on Vaupel collected material, wrote to archives and tried to find eyewitnesses. According to the teacher, the results are clear: At Hess. Lichtenau there was a larger satellite camp of Buchenwald. It was not an extermination camp, but one Labor camp.

Why now?

Vaupel on the HNA: 'It is surprising why the connection did not appear earlier. The topic has not yet been processed'. According to the research by Vaupel became the Hess external command. Lichtenau of Buchenwald concentration camp first mentioned in documents on August 2, 1944.

Factory built

The construction of the ammunition plant of Dynamit Nobel AG had already started in 1936. It was called 'Moor's Head Factory' by the residents. With 200 hectares and 360 factory buildings, the company was a huge facility. Initially, those who were on duty were employed, later prisoners of war. Up to 15,000 people were said to have worked in Hirschhagen during the war. They were housed in a wreath of camps that extended to today's Kassel district (Eschenstruth, Waldhof).

Cranking

'When attempts were made towards boosting the production of the entire defense industry even more towards the end of the war, Jews eventually became women used in the ammunition plant. They were in the Vereinshaus camp in Hess. Lichtenau housed', says Vaupel's work.

Location

The barracks stood on a site between Heinrichstrasse and Hopfelder Strasse. At first foreign construction workers lived here, later part of the SS camp was used for female prisoners, mostly Hungarian Jews, made available. The investigation later revealed that the entire camp was transferred to the SS. There are different representations about the strength of the external command. According to the 'International

Camp Committee' in March 1945 there were said to be exactly 1002 prisoners.

Eyewitnesses

Interviewed eyewitnesses testified that the Jews had to live and work in miserable conditions. Every day they were taken four kilometers to work in Hirschhagen. The Jews are mainly supposed to be in the filling stations bottling the explosive Pikrin in grenades and plate mines. The use of the substance Pikrin led to serious illnesses and even fatal liver damage in the prisoners.

Deaths

A total of 150 deaths are said to have occurred in the concentration camp external command, mostly as a result of industrial accidents in the factory. The command was evacuated on March 29, 1945, when the Americans were already in Melsungen. The inmates were led to Wurzen via Dresden and Leipzig, where they were liberated by US troops less than a month later.

Author Vaupel does not want to leave the work alone. 'History must not only be researched, it must also be made visible.' Vaupel thinks of an exhibition, publications and a memorial – a memorial of a dark past ...

Traces

Incidentally, the first, albeit vague, references to the concentration camp outpost existed in 1981. The former Oberrieder pastor Dietmar Hahn found traces of that time. Hahn back then: 'It is not so easy to ignore what happened around Hirschhagen until 1945.'

∗∗∗

After the newspaper article appeared the telephone calls began. Dieter Vaupel remembers receiving 20-30 calls. Many were supportive and said it was time to finally deal with this part of our story. They showed empathy for the terrible fate of the Hungarian Jews.

But there were also numerous negative reactions. A caller accused Dieter of wanting to throw dirt at Hessisch Lichtenau and he should stop talking about that era. Everything was gone and forgotten. One woman said Dieter should let the past go, and that the women from Hungary had a good time here and were happy to be here.

On one call, when Dieter said 'hello,' one man answered with 'SS-Sturmbannführer' and told Dieter to stay out of it and not dig in the dirt anymore, otherwise something would happen to him and his family. Another aggressive caller insulted Dieter, calling him a 'snot boy' and told him to stay out of it if he did not want anything to happen to him.

There were also professional repercussions for Dieter. He had applied for a management position at the school in Hessisch Lichtenau and his principal made it clear that he was not the right person. Dieter was being discussed too negatively in the town, having stirred up too much through his historical work.

The negative reactions, however, did not prevent Dieter and the students from continuing to meet once a week. They decided that their next undertaking would be a public presentation in February of what they had learned. They would invite all of Hessisch Lichtenau.

***

While Dieter Vaupel and the students held their weekly after-school sessions that autumn, they were unaware of a visit from another seeker of their town's past. In September 1983, only two months before publication of the newspaper article, Judith Magyar Isaacson, one of the Hungarian women sent from Auschwitz to Hessisch Lichtenau when she was a teenager, came to verify her memories for a memoir she was writing. She was accompanied by her husband Irving Isaacson, a former intelligence officer in the United States Army whom she met and married after the war. Judith, who had earned degrees in mathematics in the United States, taught at Bates College in Maine before becoming a Dean there.

She had located old barracks and a few factory buildings. But when she told locals she was looking for the underground munitions factory where she had laboured, she was told that no such place existed and to stop looking. Judith and her husband returned to the United States with no confirmation of her memories.

In retrospect, Dieter Vaupel is convinced that Judith Isaacson was not the only Jewish survivor from Lager Vereinshaus to return to validate her memories before his and the students' research became public. On 27 February 1987, Rosalia Valyi, who had been in Lager Vereinshaus too, wrote to Dieter.

> On one occasion we went to Hessisch Lichtenau, but we were unable to get any information about where the camp was located. Obviously they didn't want to remember. And because everything has changed

so much since then, we couldn't see anything. I have regretted the trip very much, as it opens up the old wounds that I thought were already healed.

Dieter also had no idea that Kati Kellner Salcer, another survivor of Lager Vereinshaus, who was then residing with her husband in New York City, never talked about the camp and the factory, and not only because it stirred up terrible memories. No one had believed Kati's story of this vast underground munitions factory with thousands of workers, not even her own husband who attributed it to traumatic memory. How could such a place exist, he wondered, when there is no historical record? It was easier for Kati to never talk about it.

The work of Dieter Vaupel and the students would profoundly impact the Jewish women and girls who survived Lager Vereinshaus, and they in turn would impact the people of Hessisch Lichtenau.

8

———

Going Public

Meeting once a week since their school's Open House in April, by December 1983 Dieter Vaupel and his students had made significant inroads with their research into the Jewish women and girls held in Lager Vereinshaus. A November article about their work in the local newspaper had brought in more than fifteen phone calls and a number of letters that offered new information and leads.

Then in early December, Dieter and the students received an astounding letter in answer to an enquiry they had made to the Central Office of the State Justice Administrations in Ludwigsburg, the main agency in Germany for investigating Nazi war crimes. The letter revealed that there had been a formal investigation into the killing of prisoners in Lager Vereinshaus in Hessisch Lichtenau. The investigation began in 1967 from Ludwigsburg, and was then conducted from the public prosecutor's office in Kassel until it was terminated in 1976.

According to the letter, the Vereinshaus camp held an average of 900 women, guarded by 25 SS men and 40 SS women. The investigators questioned former prisoners from the camp who could be located as well as former members of the SS security team. The investigation focused on camp manager Kommandofuhrer Wilhelm Schäfer and his deputy for the killing of prisoners. They were also accused of sending sick and pregnant prisoners back to Auschwitz to be murdered there.

Dieter immediately replied that he was interested in knowing more. That same month, he was allowed to view the files on the investigation in Ludwigsburg, and then in January of 1984 he went through the files in Kassel. He was especially intrigued by the Jewish women and girls' descriptions of their living and working conditions in the camp. He also learned that the investigation was terminated by the public prosecutor's office in Kassel in 1976 because the camp's manager Wilhelm Schäfer could no longer be found and the identity of the deputy remained unknown.

A few years later Dieter Vaupel would carry out a more detailed analysis as part of his doctoral dissertation and show that some of the investigations were superficial at best. Little effort had been put into determining where Kommandofuhrer Willi Schäfer was living at the time. It had also been claimed that Schäfer's deputy could not be identified. However, from the survivor interviews and records, Dieter Vaupel was able to easily determine that this man was SS Obercharfuhrer Ernst Zorbach, who still lived in Essen in the 1990s.

✳✳✳

Dieter Vaupel left the public prosecutor's office in Kassel armed with a list of the addresses of some of the Jewish women and girls who had been interviewed. To have the names and addresses of women and girls whose fate he and his students had been chasing for the past ten months made their hard work well worth it. Dieter told them he would write to all the women on the list.

Dieter informed the local newspaper of what he had learned from the investigative files and on 3 January 1984, HNA ran an article entitled, 'Justice confirms information about concentration camp external command'.

After the article appeared, Dieter received ten phone calls and three letters. One Hessisch Lichtenau resident told Dieter about having helped three Jewish women escape from the camp, and provided a thank-you letter dated 8 April 1947.

These women had escaped under a fence from Lager Vereinshaus, ran into the forest and were never found. Later in his research Dieter would discover they had stayed hidden in the forest until American troops had captured Hessisch Lichtenau on 2 April 1945. After the Americans came they lived with a family in Fürstenhagen until mid-May.

On 18 January 1984, HNA carried a follow-up article on Dieter and the students' research, 'Don't sweep historical truth under the carpet'. Vaupel, it was reported, had received calls and letters since the 3 January HNA article: 'The positive reactions had dominated, but threats against the author had also been made: One should stay out and do not dig in the dirt.'

Speaking about those who contacted him, Dieter said: 'Callers and also letter writers made it clear how much help the Jewish women and workers in the factory received (despite the threat of severe punishment) from the Lichtenau population and workers (giving food and throwing them clothes). Certainly some of these women would not have survived the camp time without this help.'

Dieter also made it clear that he was not interested in using the names of people from Hessisch Lichtenau in the book he planned on writing, an issue he knew was a concern in the town. His goal was to learn about the Jewish women and girls and determine their fate.

Mayor Ingo Geisler of Hessisch Lichtenau was also quoted in the article: 'The topic is now in the public domain and must be discussed. We cannot sweep the historical truth under the carpet.' At the same time, the mayor publicly voiced concern over people having their reputations permanently damaged if the historical material were evaluated in the 'wrong way,' Geisler said. 'Everyone is touched by the topic,' also noting that how the memories of the victims of the Nazi era should be kept alive also needed to be discussed.

***

Dieter's work continued to remain divisive in the town. The publicity intensified the debate about the findings, with many people voicing skepticism and doubt. Dieter and the students decided it was time to get the facts out and publicly present their research results.

Together they also decided that given the heated nature of the topic, the students would attend but Dieter alone would speak. Dieter knew that the facts had to be presented in a clear and concise way and without editorializing. None of the students felt comfortable doing this.

Dieter and the students soon hit a roadblock in planning a public presentation: it was impossible to find a venue. The school auditorium was not an option as school management deemed their work too divisive and the mayor was not forthcoming. Then Dr. Ernst Froehlich, Chairman of the Reichenbach Castle Association, approached Dieter. The Reichenbach Castle Association was a group of citizens dedicated to the local history of Reichenbach, a district of Hessisch Lichtenau about two kilometers from town.

Dr. Froehlich believed that the munitions factory in Hirschhagen and the concentration camp subcamp right in the middle of Hessisch Lichtenau should not be erased from history. A public presentation was scheduled to take place in Reichenbach on 10 February 1984. It would be held in the local history museum housed in an old building next to the village church called Sippelscher Hof, a house once owned by the Sippel family.

Dieter's father, Karl Vaupel, had grown up in Reichenbach. Dieter's paternal ancestors had long-standing roots in Reichenbach, with his grandfather and grandmother living there all their lives. Dieter's grandfather had a small farm and was the local wainwright, making and repairing wooden harvest wagons, handcarts and wooden wheels. He had also served as mayor of the small village.

Only days before the scheduled presentation, Dieter received a package from Auschwitz in response to the inquiry he had made. Auschwitz sent a 17-page list with the names of all women sent to Hessisch Lichtenau, as well as further documents about the SS guards, and the return transport of 206 women from Hessisch Lichtenau who were immediately gassed upon arrival at Auschwitz.

Dieter shared the information from Auschwitz with HNA. The newspaper ran an article on 8 February 1984: 'Documents from Poland supplement research on the external command of the concentration camp from Hess. Lichtenau "transferred" to Auschwitz.'

If one looked at the correspondence between the SS command at Hessisch Lichtenau and the administration at Buchenwald, Dieter told the newspaper, there was a certain horror in its objectivity: 'Even the extermination of people had to be done according to regulations.'

The article went on to describe the documents Dieter had received from Auschwitz, including a letter that described women from the Hirschhagen area being called to a training course to become SS helpers at the Vereinshaus camp. They were to be used for supervisory and care services for the Jews. These women had no choice in this selection.

***

As the presentation date approached, the controversy and threats continued. Dieter was still being told to leave the past alone, that nobody cares anymore. One caller even told the married teacher with two young sons that he should 'keep his fingers out of it' or something will happen to him and his family. Dieter did not take the threats seriously, until the day before the presentation.

One of the students from the group came in and told Dieter that people from where he lived in Fürstenhagen, a district of Hessisch Lichtenau, had announced that they would come and beat Dieter up that evening.

This warning seemed very specific, and for the first time Dieter was afraid that it might be real. He thought about cancelling the event. Not knowing what he should do, Dieter turned to his father for advice. He had always had a close relationship with his father Karl. They had many discussions over the years. Even during the student movement of 1968 when there was a lot of generational conflict and Dieter was wearing his hair long and questioning authority, he and his father kept talking even if they did not always agree. They always respected each other's opinion.

Dieter told his father about his fears over doing the presentation. He was conflicted over what to do. Would it be cowardly to cancel? He knew he was lucky to live in a democracy where the legal system would protect him. Look at how many people were intimidated, arrested and mistreated during the Nazi era because of their different opinions.

Karl Vaupel told his son words he has never forgotten: 'Nothing will happen to you. I'll come with you tonight, so you don't have to go there alone.'

***

The HNA wrote about the presentation in an article from 11 February 1984: 'First round of discussions about concentration camp external command/Different echo obtained from the past.' The paper reported that Dr. Ernst Froehlich, who was the first to take the risk of publicly discussing the explosive topic, made the introduction before the well-attended event.

Dr. Froehlich told the audience that we want to know what was really going on in Hessisch Lichtenau, adding, 'You have to strive for historical truth.'

During his prepared talk and slide show Dieter presented the facts from the investigative files and Auschwitz, but also discussed how the Jewish women and girls received acts of kindness from Hessisch Lichtenau citizens who gave them food and clothing in spite of the risk to their own lives.

Reactions to Dieter's presentation were mixed. HNA reported:

> While younger citizens tended to seek immediate clarification of the city's recent history, reports have been met with outrage from older Lichtenauers. Dark memories are awakened, people fear for the reputation of the city. Should all of this really be stirred up again? The question sounded through in the discussion. An older citizen even warned against putting a memorial stone to the Jews who died in Lichtenau. You shouldn't pollute your own nest. It was also bad elsewhere in the terrible Nazi era.

One attendee suggested that a memorial plaque should not only be erected for the Jews but for all the victims of the Third Reich in Hessisch Lichtenau. Why should the Jews get special treatment? In at least three accidents in the explosives plant, there were a total of 200 deaths.

Someone pointed out there were contradictions in Dieter's research. Was it 800 or 1,000 Jews? How can we believe your data? Indeed, such calculations met with little understanding. However, one audience member commented, 'Whether it was 800, 1,000 or just 300 Jews, it was bad enough.'

Dr. Froehlich ended the evening by saying that he accepted Dieter Vaupel's version of the events but one should also put it into perspective.

'Hessisch Lichtenau was not an extermination camp, but a labour camp. According to his findings, Jews were never shot. And he also doubted the existence of a gallows in the camp.'

Afterwards, when people came up to Dieter, he did not know what to expect, but he knew his father was here. He was relieved when the people said they supported his research. After some discussion they came up with the idea to start a history project with interested members of the community. No one threatened or tried to beat up Dieter that night.

***

After finding addresses of survivors from Lager Vereinshaus in the investigative files in Kassel, Dieter Vaupel did write to the women. He received his first reply shortly after his public presentation. Sabine Gross wrote to Dieter in March 1984, and then Esther Fuchs in April 1984. Both women were now living in Israel.

Sabine Gross
March 2, 1984
Haifa/Israel

Dear Mr Dieter Vaupel,

Thank you for your kind letter of January 31, 1984. I wonder where you got my address from?

I will soon be 80 years old and my memory is not that good anymore, but I will write you everything I can remember.

In June 1944, when I was 40 years old, I was deported to Auschwitz from the Ghetto Satmar. I was stripped naked by SS men and all my head and body hair was cut off with an electric shaving machine. Then I was allowed to put on some old clothes that were only rags, but without underwear.

We women were beaten with sticks and kicked, and had to stand for hours. We got so little and such bad food to eat that we were all always hungry and terribly emaciated and exhausted.

After the transfer to Hess. Lichtenau to the 'Vereinshaus' camp, we had to walk uphill and downhill to work every day for a long time. (Cement factory in Fürstenhagen). From early in the morning until 4 in the afternoon I had to carry heavy pieces of concrete. All of my legs are so damaged that I am disabled and you can still see the scars on my back from wearing the concrete pieces.

It was very cold towards the end of January 1945. Nevertheless, we had to walk to work as usual. My left side of my face was frozen and I developed an inflammation of the nerve that is still incurable to this day. All my teeth had to be pulled.

The meal consisted of a thin slice of very bad bread and a few slices of potatoes. This had to be enough for both breakfast and lunch. When we got back from work we got a thin bad soup.

Then we had to stand Apell. Until seven o'clock in the evening, then we were released into the cold and damp barrack and there were many rats.

In early May 1945 we were liberated by western troops.

I can no longer tell you because I have forgotten a lot and do not want to think about this terrible time. But I hope to have given your young generation a small picture of the time. My fate was, despite all the suffering, not as severe as that of many others who have been cruelly tortured and murdered.

Sabine Gross

Esther Fuchs
April 24, 1984
Kiriat Ono/Israel

Dear Mr Vaupel,

In response to your letter, I can say the following: after 40 years, it is hard and bitter to think about it. Only four of the family with nine children stayed alive. Fascism killed our souls after being sent to Auschwitz. As if we had no name and no family, they gave us the name SAUJUDE! Yes, that's how it started!

As answers to your questions, I will tell you the following:

1. A short time after delivery in Auschwitz, we were in wagons and transported to Hessisch-Lichtenau.

2. From the train station, the SS guards chased us into the Hessisch-Lichtenau concentration camp, I can remember a large gate. This did not happen without a beating and the insult 'Saujude!'

3. At first sight we saw that the camp was much better equipped than Auschwitz. We thought the barracks were clean, we had bunks and

the main thing was water. We could drink and clean up. Our own equipment was miserable, we had rags as clothes and clogs, no underwear at all. The diet was also very poor. Broth of water with 50 grams of bread a day. We had to work hard with it, 10-12 hours a day.

4. There was a camp leader named Willi in the camp, he made the daily appeal and plagued us with various things. He let us rest for hours in the rain, cold and wind. The SS guards and SS guards beat, insulted and plagued us.

Once the one named Willi wanted every tenth of us to be shot dead. He said that a security guard found a piece of meat that we wanted to steal, we Sau-Jewish whores, I don't know if it's true. The main thing was that they could torture us mentally. The SS guards were sadists, rude and took advantage of us every moment to torture, beat and abuse. They made a sport out of those who are rude and inhumane.

5. The way to work: The workplace was far away, they put us in the train station and we took the train for a while. Then we were unloaded and walked about 1½ hours and the same thing back. With such living conditions that we had and 10 to 12 hours of work a day, it was very difficult. The jobs were in the forest and in the ammunition factory. I can remember that once there was a lot of snow, we couldn't go with our wooden soled shoes as fast as the guards wanted. The SS team and the SS guards beat us and scolded the whole flat. They kicked us to work and kicked us and beat us – then we had to work for ten hours. We were afraid of going back to the camp.

6. As I have already noticed, the jobs were in the ammunition factory and in the forest. We dug a water outlet in the forest and chopped and stacked wood. We stacked and packed grenades in the ammunition factory. Once a grenade fell on my foot, but I had to continue working without medical attention until the wound healed by itself.

7. In October 1944, foreign SS men came to our camp and, together with the SS guards and SS guards, chased all the sick out of the so-called sick area. Afterwards, they still came to the camp and also have many from there with them dragged the sick away. We didn't know where to.

We only heard that 206 women were selected and liquidated at that time. The SS made the so-called selection without a doctor and examination, beat and torture, inhumane and sadistic.

8. A man named step-dad beat me bloody and kicked me in the body because I hadn't stood still as he wanted. This was a way to let off the sadistic soul of the SS. The other SS men and SS guards also used every moment to torture us and beat us and kill our souls.

9. Evacuation: We set off from the camp on a train to Leipzig. There we were unloaded and hunted back and forth on foot because the American and Russian armies were all around Leipzig. We walked there without eating and drinking, in the cold and rain. The SS men and guards were rude and sadists to the very last moment. From day to day there were fewer SS and guards with us. They fled 'heroically!'

Finally, in the city of Wurzen, the Americans liberated us, took us to the barracks there, gave us food, clothing and medical care. After a while the Czechs got us into the car and brought us to the Czech city of Nachod. We went home from there.

10. Unfortunately I don't have any papers or photographs from that time, so I can't send you anything.

In conclusion: My dear sir, you cannot imagine yourself in our lives. What it meant to me when I arrived home and learned the bitter truth that father, mother and five brothers and sisters did not come back from this hell. Can you imagine the blissful state we were left in? We always lived in our little village, father made charcoal in the forest and sold it from house to house in town so we had food and our modest maintenance.

Since I don't speak German, I told my brother-in-law everything. He also went through hell and after 1945 he didn't want to speak, write or read German anymore. I told him to write this letter.

Esther Fuchs

9

Geschichtswerkstatt

In response to the commotion stirred up by Dieter Vaupel's public presentation, Ingo Geisler, the mayor of Hessisch Lichtenau, appointed a formal working group. They were tasked with researching the history of the munitions factory and the associated camps with two historians hired to eventually report the committee's results. Some townspeople, however, wanted to move much faster to make sure the Nazi era was not again forgotten.

This grassroots movement by local citizens began soon after Dieter's talk. Two townspeople, Jürgen Jessen and Gisela Höfert, volunteered for the effort. Jürgen lived with his family in Hessisch Lichtenau and taught in a school in Witzenhausen, a town twenty kilometers away. Gisela Höfert was a Lichtenauer whose mother had been one of the more than 2,000 Germans required to work at Hirschhagen.

By 1985, their group numbered about ten, including Dieter, and they took the first steps to form an enduring history workshop or 'Geschichtswerkstatt', with the goal of promoting remembrance. Their first effort would be a memorial stone for the Jewish women and girls to be installed on the grounds of the former Vereinshaus camp where a primary school, a kindergarten and a part of the Freiherr-vom-Stein-Schule now stood.

The history group knew it would not be easy to gain support for this proposal. Many in the town were adamant that Jews were not the only ones who had suffered during the Nazi regime, so why should they be the only ones remembered with a monument?

Relying on Dieter and the Project Week students' research, along with the research gathered by Dieter for his scholarly articles and 1984 book on the Jewish women and girls, the history group strove to convince others that the suffering of the Jews was far greater than that of forced labourers from other countries.

The research revealed that the Nazis imposed a demonstrable hierarchy in their treatment of the workers at Hirschhagen. Not surprisingly, at the top were the German workers. German men were brought in as construction workers and German women came to the factory as part of their required

Figure 11: German employees, Hirschhagen, early 1940s. Private Archive Dieter Vaupel.

Figure 12: Dutch men and German civil servant girlfriends, Hirshhagen, early 1940s. Private Archive Dieter Vaupel.

national service. These young women were German civil servants known as Dienstverpflichteten.

Below the Germans, next in the hierarchy, were the so-called western workers – the Belgians, Dutch and French. They were afforded protective gear, fed well enough to sustain themselves, and were even given time off to relax and socialize in their 'Sunday best'.

Poles and prisoners of war from the Soviet Union were considered barely one step up from the Jews, who were at the very bottom of the worker hierarchy. The Nazis labelled these workers to easily differentiate them from other forced labourers; the Russians had an 'OST' badge sewn on their clothes and the Poles a 'P'.

The Russians and Poles lived under miserable conditions similar to that of the Jewish women and girls. In the Esche camp in Eschenstruth, Russian women and girls were overworked and underfed, lived among vermin and without heat in the winter.

It was strictly forbidden to take photographs of the Russian and Polish forced labourers. One photo taken does show a Russian girl named Natasia, who was used as a forced labourer on a farm in Hessisch Lichtenau, holding the farmer's son in her arms.

The Jewish women and girls sent to Hessisch Lichtenau lived under conditions similar to the Poles and Russians but with added horrors. They were under the constant threat of being sent back to Auschwitz to be gassed. For no apparent reason, the SS guards might kick, punch, whip or hit them with heavy sticks. The Jewish women and girls were also assigned the most dangerous jobs in the factory.

✷✷✷

The 1,000 Jewish women and girls from Auschwitz were sent to the munitions factory after a call came in saying workers were needed. They were counted and lined up before they were put on cattle cars for Hessisch Lichtenau. These women and girls were among the over 430,000 Jews transported to Auschwitz from Hungary in 1944. Thousands of these women and girls would work in the German arms industry. The munitions factory in Hessisch Lichtenau was only one such destination.

After over a year of many debates and much discussion, the history group finally succeeded; their proposal for a memorial stone for the Jewish woman and girls received unanimous approval from all the political parties in the city parliament of Hessisch Lichtenau.

But as the local newspaper HNA reported on 19 June 1985, the city did make a concession to those who were upset that the memorial was only for the Jewish workers. 'In addition, the city committees want to consider further considerations for a memorial in Hessisch Lichtenau for the victims of war and violence.' (It would be almost 15 years before a memorial was erected commemorating the 178 forced workers from different nations killed in explosions at the factory.)

The inauguration ceremony for the memorial stone took place on 24 April 1986. Around 150 invited guests attended. Fully aware of the disputes about the monument, Mayor Geisler wanted to keep the event local, so there were only a few guests from outside the area. These included representatives from the Jewish community in Kassel and the Society for Christian-Jewish Cooperation. The police were also present to prevent neo-Nazis from disrupting the event. In an article headlined, 'Memorial for Jewish women. Inauguration simple and dignified', (26 April 1986) HNA reported Mayor Ingo Geisler as saying:

> With this stone as a symbol of remembrance we want to express our inner willingness to show due respect to the Jewish women and girls who have suffered here in our city…It is not about…to what extent

Figure 13: Memorial Inscription, site of former Lager Vereinshaus Hessisch Lichtenau, 1986. Photo by Dieter Vaupel.

each individual citizen was jointly responsible for this horrific mistake by the people. Rather, it is important that we all…agree that respect for life, dignity and human rights is equally due to everyone.

At the dedication, Dieter Vaupel spoke about the harsh daily life of the Jewish women and girls in the camp and the factory. He also talked about the courageous Lichtenauers who at great risk threw clothes, shoes, bread and cake over the camp fence or surreptitiously handed the women and girls something as they were marched to work.

One group of uninvited guests, possibly young people who looked to be part of a peace movement, stood quietly on the edge of the memorial. The neo-Nazis stayed away.

[Translation of Memorial] In memory of the Hungarian Jewish women who suffered here from 2.8.1944 to 29.3.1945 as prisoners in the Hess. Lichtenau external command of the Buchenwald concentration camp.

***

The memorial stone had been a contentious issue, but not nearly as contentious as the history workshop's next project: Bringing together former German workers, the former forced foreign labourers and the Jewish woman and girls from Lager Vereinshaus for a three-day meeting in Hessisch Lichtenau.

10

Talks, Tours and Tears

The idea to invite former German and foreign workers from the munitions factory to Hessisch Lichtenau for a meeting originated with Gisela Höfert, a member of the history workshop. Gisela, whose mother Minna Schiffer was required to work at the factory for five years as a young woman, had heard many stories about that horrid place. Minna told her daughter about the hardships she had suffered, but also of how much worse it had been for the foreign forced labourers and the Jews.

Gisela's mother also spoke of how the factory workers had promised each other that when the war was over they would all come back to Hessisch Lichtenau. So Gisela proposed that the town invite all the workers, the Germans, Belgians, Dutch, French, Russians and Poles, and the Hungarian Jews sent from Auschwitz. They would ask everyone from the factory to come, except of course the ex-SS and any Germans who had volunteered for duty at the factory.

Such a meeting was a radical idea with possible downsides. This could not be some sort of happy school reunion, where people would raise a glass and clap each other on the back while recalling all the good times they had together, with some even encountering sweethearts from their youth. And what if they did, what if these old workers, the Germans, Belgians, Dutch and French, were happy to see each other? How would this seem to those who had suffered great deprivations, the Russians and Polish forced labourers, and of course the Jewish women and girls sent from Auschwitz, who endured the worst of all? Why bring these people together? What was the purpose?

For the history workshop, the purpose was to give these people the chance to exchange memories, revive old contacts and rework a piece of German history. But would they want to come? The solution, it seemed, was to see if they would like the opportunity to come back to Hessisch Lichtenau.

Dieter Vaupel already had some names and addresses of Jewish girls and women that he found in the investigative files in Ludwigsberg and Kassel. And he had discovered another trove of names and addresses after Benjamin Ferencz, the American lawyer who was a chief prosecutor of Nazi war crimes, suggested that he contact the Jewish Claims Conference in Frankfurt. He would write to the Jewish women and girls.

Both Jürgen Jessen and Gisela Höfert had been gathering names and addresses of the German and foreign forced labourers, and now Gisela's mother Minna offered to help. Jürgen Jessen volunteered to take the lead in securing possible funding for a meeting, while Dieter would be responsible for the historical content to be presented. They had an organizational structure in place; the next step was to secure the support of the town, through Mayor Ingo Geisler.

The mayor of Hessisch Lichtenau, as expected, dismissed the idea immediately. Had he not already allowed the installation of a memorial stone to the Jews? Had he not appointed a formal working group, which included professors of history as well as Dieter Vaupel, to study the history of the factory? And now this so-called history project, this group of citizens who were at best amateur historians, wanted to bring ex-workers here to Lichtenau? Unthinkable.

The history workshop was not to be deterred. Dieter recognized that the mayor was not necessarily opposed to coming to terms with the history of the Nazis and hosting the meeting. But the mayor was a politician and did not like when things moved too quickly and out of his control. Mostly he did not want to put on an event that could draw too much attention and damage the reputation of Hessisch Lichtenau.

Not satisfied with the mayor's 'no', the history workshop persisted. They decided the best strategy to advocate for their proposal was through the press. They contacted the local newspaper, and were pleased when the coverage increased public support for the town holding such a gathering. Then the mayor's formal working group received some bad publicity when Prof Dr. Dietfrid-Krause-Villmar of the University of Kassel, an eminent scholar of National Socialism, resigned from the group, in protest that the town was not taking the search for the historical truth seriously.

When Jürgen Jessen received initial funding from the State of Hesse and the German government to help support the ex-workers reunion, Mayor Ingo Geisler and his Christian Democratic Union (CDU) party had to give in. The mayor relented and the city parliament, with the votes of the CDU, the Social Democratic Party (SPD) and the German Communist Party (DKP), passed a unanimous decision to provide the financial means for the meeting. The gathering was scheduled for the 3-5 October 1986.

In reaction to the good news, Gisela told HNA in a 20 August 1986 article entitled 'Program for the first meeting of former forced laborers is available', that 'the response to this meeting has been extremely positive for those affected. Many are grateful that even after 40 years they still remember them and their fate and give them the opportunity to meet other alumni'.

However, the article also noted that Mayor Geisler and Ms Höfert 'did not hide that the announcement of the meeting also triggered negative reactions in town with some of the opinion that the past should finally be left alone'. They also emphasized that the meeting was in no way about blaming someone or settling the blame.

Funds were promised from the city of Hessisch Lichtenau, the District of Kassel, the State of Hesse and the German state to cover the costs for the invited guests, which was DM 15,000. Guests would be accommodated privately by citizens of Hessisch Lichtenau in their homes, the beginning of many long-standing friendships between townspeople and returnees. The vast majority of those invited gratefully accepted the opportunity to come and talk about what had happened.

***

Figure 14: Left to right: Iósza Ignácz, Klara Bohm, Ibolya Méth, Magdalena Kornfein, Henriette Szepes. Photo by Dieter Vaupel.

One hundred former workers from the munitions factory came to Hessisch Lichtenau for the October 1986 meeting. There were German workers, Dutch and French forced workers, and a delegation of five Jewish women from Hungary.

The three-day event was packed with tours, talks and many tears. Sometimes these were tears of joy, as when Frenchman Jean Eclàche encountered his former German girlfriend. There were also tears of sadness. Jean had worked with Jewish women and girls as they struggled to load the heavy bombs onto railroad cars.

For Jean and some of the Jewish women their tears of sadness were also mixed with great pride. Jean was among the forced workers who had shown some of the Jewish women and girls how to sabotage the weapons. Specifically, he showed them how to make the detonators on the bombs unusable. Many of the Jewish women and girls reported sabotaging wherever possible. They knew it was risking their lives but it made them feel better to do something about the war and save lives.

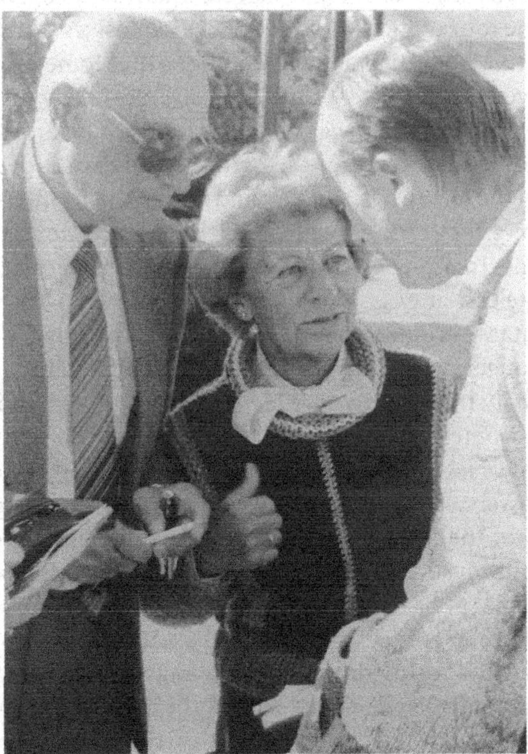

Figure 15: Jean Eclàche with Ibola Mèth and the translator. Private Archive Dieter Vaupel.

It was an especially poignant reunion when Jean Eclàche encountered Ibola Mèth, one of the Hungarian Jewish girls who he had taught how to sabotage bombs.

Fears that it would be problematic to bring ex-workers of the factory together as some were treated much more harshly because of their backgrounds prove unfounded. Their common traumatic experience proved to be a deep and unspoken bond.

In addition to the local newspaper HNA, the event drew interest from national press from all over the Federal Republic of Germany. The *TAZ Berlin*, *Frankfurter Rundschau*, *Die Zeit* and *Der Stern* and other magazines reported on the meeting. Internationally, news reports appeared in France, Holland, Hungary and Israel.

The *Frankfurter Rundschau*, in 'Where women had to fill an explosive device' (7 October 1986), reported on the ex-workers tour of the site of the former munitions factory:

> The Jews in particular remained silent and calm when the buses turned into the forest of Hirschhagen...Many had slept badly the night before the tour of the site of the former explosives factory 'because of the difficult memories' and the 'emotions that come up', were nervous and moved...The filling of the explosive devices, which was mainly carried out by women, was one of the most dangerous in the entire plant, not least because of the extremely high risk of explosion. By handling the chemicals, the skin and hair of the women turned yellow to green: a fact that earned them the name 'Canaries'...The most inhumane treatment was given to the Jewish forced labourers... 'Nevertheless, it was lucky for us to come to Hirschhagen. In Auschwitz we would probably have been gassed just like our family,' says a Hungarian...Today it is an 'inner need' for her to return to these places that she has only terrible memories of. All contact between German women and foreign forced labourers was...strictly prohibited at the time. Nevertheless, the Jews were occasionally given something to eat or were addressed. On the way and when walking through the grounds of the former factory in the Hirschhagen forest, when the warm autumn sun seemed almost forgiving, they still hardly spoke to each other.

In his speech at the closing of the meeting, Mayor Ingo Geisler remarked: 'It was not hate and revenge that caused the meeting, but the need for memory. Not the enemy was sought, but the friend and helper from back then.'

The attendees thanked those who had invited them. They were glad they had come. The history workshop decided to repeat the event the next year, and scheduled the next meeting for the 3–6 September 1987.

***

Thanks to the press coverage of the meeting in Europe and Israel, the history workshop heard from other ex-workers. However, this coverage did not reach the United States. This explains why Judith Isaacson was shocked to receive a package at Bates College, where she was a Dean. In it was a scholarly paper by a German named Dieter Vaupel about the 1,000 Hungarian Jewish women and girls send from Auschwitz to Hessisch Lichtenau to work in a munitions factory.

Judith and her husband had visited Hessisch Lichtenau in September 1983 in search of the factory where she had been sent as a forced labourer during the war. At the time she was told such a place never existed and that she should stop looking. Now here was an academic paper explaining that the factory had been owned by Dynamit Nobel, the Nobel family, and was one of the largest munitions factories of the Deutsche Reich, in fact one of the largest munitions factories in all Europe.

Judith immediately contacted Dieter and they began a correspondence. Dieter had left his high school teaching job and started a new position in the autumn of 1986 as a lecturer at the University of Kassel while pursuing his doctorate in political science. The topic of his dissertation was the Hungarian Jewish women and girls of Hessisch Lichtenau.

Of particular note, in one letter Judith mentioned Luciana Nissim, who was the medic for the Jewish women and girls in Hessisch Lichtenau. Luciana was an Italian of the Jewish faith who arrived with two nurses to the Vereinshaus camp shortly after the transport of the 1,000 women and girls from Auschwitz.

Thanks to Judith's letter Luciana would be invited to the 1987 meeting. She would attend, as would Judith, who would stay in the home of Dieter's parents, Martha and Karl Vaupel.

11

───

Remember, But How?

Since Project Week of 1983, Dieter Vaupel had been researching the fate of the Jewish women and girls sent to Hessisch Lichtenau from Auschwitz. At first he did this on his own and together with his students, then as part of both the town's formal working group and its citizen-led history workshop. Remarkably for a high school teacher, he wrote articles that were published in scholarly journals. And in 1984, his book about the women and girls of Hirschhagen was published as part of a series on the history of German National Socialism. His research became more formalized when he left teaching school in 1986 to pursue his Ph.D. The Jewish women and girls would be the subject of his doctoral dissertation.

Dieter had more than a scholarly interest in the fate of these women and girls. He certainly felt that bringing them back to Hessisch Lichtenau for a reunion was a good first step. But the more he learned about the women, the more he wanted to help bring them recognition and justice. In meeting and corresponding, he realized how important it was for their story to be told, that people knew what they had to suffer. Dieter thought this was particularly important for the women who returned to Hungary after the war. They had little opportunity to talk about what had happened to them. To avoid stigma and prejudice in that post-war society, they had to hide that they had been in concentration camps, and even that they were Jews.

Perhaps, Dieter thought, compensation for their suffering might afford these women the recognition and justice he believed they deserved. For advice, Dieter wrote to Benjamin Ferencz, the Hungarian-born American lawyer who had been an investigator of Nazi war crimes and chief prosecutor of one of the twelve United States military trials held at Nuremberg. After the trial, Benjamin Ferencz fought for compensation for their suffering and the restitution of property for survivors. In early 1986 he suggested Dieter contact the Jewish Claims Conference (JCC).

In Frankfurt, the JCC's director, Dr. Ernst Katzenstein, enthusiastically welcomed Dieter, giving him full access to the files on compensation for the forced workers at the munitions factory. Dieter learned of the ten years of unsuccessful negotiations with the representative of Friedrich Flick, owner of Dynamit Nobel AG, of which the Hessisch Lichtenau factory was a subsidiary. Through Dr. Katzenstein, Dieter contacted Gershon Cohn, a lawyer with Israel's restitution organization, who invited Dieter to come to Israel to meet survivors of the munitions factory, and research files in the archives of the Claims Conference and Yad Vashem.

Dieter accepted the invitation but had mixed feelings about the trip. He was looking forward to meeting many survivors there, but at the same time, he did not know how they would react to him as a German, someone from the country that had killed their families and caused them enormous suffering.

All his concerns were quickly dispelled on arrival, when he was received with an unexpected level of warmth. He soon realized that the Jewish women knew about his 1984 book, *Das Aussenkommando Hessisch Lichtenau des*

Figure 16: Some of the Jewish women who attended Haifa reception, 1987. Private Archive Dieter Vaupel.

Konzentrationslagers Buchenwald 1944-1945. The book served as an 'admission ticket' to this community for Dieter. The women were so thankful that he had documented in print what had happened to them. In years to come, their story would continue to be honoured when Dieter's book would become part of the permanent collections of such esteemed institutions as the United States Holocaust Memorial Museum in Washington, DC.

Dieter's Israel trip began with a reception in Haifa attended by 50 of the women who had survived the munitions factory.

At the reception Dieter talked about his research and how it all began with students doing a school project in the spring of 1983. Afterwards, he was showered with invitations from the women but was unable to meet them all during his three weeks in Israel. In turn, he invited them all to Hessisch Lichtenau for the upcoming September 1987 reunion meeting of workers from the munitions factory.

After the conference Dieter spent many days studying files in the archives at the Claims Conference in Tel Aviv and Yad Vashem in Jerusalem. In addition to his archive research, Dieter conducted and recorded many interviews with survivors.

Dieter was especially moved by an interview with a Mrs Weinberger from Jerusalem. Mrs Weinberger's son, who was about Dieter's age, had driven him to her home in Tel Aviv. The son sat in silence while his mother had a long conversation with Dieter. She gave moving details about her personal fate and the fate of her family, her time in Auschwitz, the work in Hessisch Lichtenau, life in the camp, and the death march they were led on when the camp was emptied at the end of the war. Afterwards the son drove Dieter back to his hotel. The son told Dieter that what his mother had just said was all new to him. She never talked about it. He thanked Dieter for coming to Israel. His work was so important. Now he could better understand much that was previously incomprehensible to him about his mother.

From this own interviews and in researching the reports by the women who survived Auschwitz and Hessisch Lichtenau, what particularly moved Dieter was when the women spoke of life after liberation. Among them, Aranka Luxemberg: 'Even today I startle from the nightmares screaming because the stress on the soul was too great.' Or Rosalya Valyi: 'I feel that the humiliations suffered there affect a whole life, that the last animal was treated better than we had been for a whole year. But in general, the circumstances, the anxiety, the fear of death and the subsequent depression have left indelible traces.'

Dieter left Israel with a profound appreciation of how important it was that these women receive some special form of moral and material reparation for what they had to endure. Later that same year, the Jewish women were finally able to receive some limited sense of this through compensation payments from the factory owners. A settlement allowed the ex-workers from the munitions factory to file claims against Dynamit Nobel AG. The compensation was largely symbolic as each woman only received a one-time payment for her forced labour of DM 2,000, and the application process was arduous. Each had to verify their presence at the factory. For every one of the women who sought compensation, Dieter would provide the verification they needed.

The trip to Israel went better than Dieter ever imagined; the one snag was at the airport before flying home. Security officers conducting a routine check before Dieter could exit the country did not know what to make of a German citizen with a suitcase full of copies of statements by Jewish women who had been in a concentration and labour camp. Dieter's suitcase was unpacked and he was questioned several times before they decided that this man was telling the truth, he was truly interested in the fates of these women and helping them receive compensation.

***

The history workshop organizers, Jürgen Jessen, Gisela Höfert and Dieter Vaupel, could not be more pleased. Where five Jewish women from the Vereinshaus camp attended the first meeting of ex-workers, 63 came to Hessisch Lichtenau for the September 1987 reunion: 40 from Hungary, 20 from Israel, two from the United States and one from Italy. In total there were almost 150 former workers.

The local newspaper HNA covered the meeting's opening night event with the headline 'Former workers interested in Lichtenau; Hope has replaced hatred' (5 September 1987).

In his welcoming remarks, the newspaper noted, Russian Michael Semirjaga's words to his fellow ex-workers were met with great applause: 'We have to fight together for peace so that there will never be forced labourers again.'

Semirjaga made the journey to Hessisch Lichtenau with fellow countryman Alexander Wassiljew, so that what happened to them would not be forgotten. Marian Szeptucho, a Pole who was brought to the factory in 1941 as a forced worker for three and a half years, was another attendee thankful for the gathering.

Vera Ausländer from Haifa, Israel, HNA also reported, found it difficult to make the trip but did not regret the long journey: 'I am glad that I came. Lichtenau has a beautiful facade, but it was bitter in the memory.' Vera also said she no longer felt hatred for Germans and hoped that with a new generation of young people that things will get better.

Two sisters who had been in the Vereinshaus camp also attended the reunion of ex-workers. Blanka Pudler, a Hungarian Jewish woman who had been brought to Hessisch Lichtenau from Auschwitz when she was barely 15 years old, came with her older sister Aranka. Blanka said she was still tormented by terrible memories and was afraid of what it would be like when she returned. She made no secret that she had a great hatred of the Germans after the war. However, she admitted that her attitude had changed over the years. 'Today's Lichtenau is no longer comparable to that of the past,' she said.

Blanka, above all, was grateful for the great interest that the Lichtenau students have shown in their fate. Martha Frank, a Jewish woman from Hungary, agreed with Blanka, noting how the children of their tormentors now had a different attitude.

Unlike the previous year, no divisive debate roiled the town about hosting the second meeting. The history workshop was therefore able to include local schoolchildren in the September 1987 gathering so they could meet and talk to the ex-workers and former concentration camp inmates. Fortuitously, the beginning of that year's Project Week at the Freiherr-vom-Stein-Schule coincided with the September 1987 meeting.

Thirteen Project Week students attended the event, led by teacher Karl Bachsleitner. Their project was researching the question: Remember, but how? How to deal with Nazi history in Hessisch Lichtenau in the future? More than once it was noted how far things had come; only four years before Project Week 1983 students were asking the question that started it all: What happened in their town during the Nazi era?

Dirk Schneider, an alumni of Project Week 1983, provided some well-received welcoming remarks. Dieter later included his words in an article in the 2005 book *Second History and Historical Education*.

With great pride Dirk Schneider told the audience:

> I would especially like to thank you for coming here. For me that is also a satisfaction. I am one of the 'late-born' and I think it's just great that finally there are also the people I have only heard of: the Hungarian Jews, of whom I only knew one report. I read that, it shook me deeply. I was also ashamed of having lived here in the city for so many years and knowing nothing about it. Nobody said anything about it. We students came across it more or less by accident. I have seen the reactions in the city and that is why I am particularly pleased that something like this meeting has now taken place here.

✳✳✳

Among the planned activities for the 1987 reunion was a visit by the Hungarian-Jewish women to the former site of Lager Vereinhaus, now home to the Freiherr-vom-Stein-Schule. The women were reminded beforehand that the site now looked nothing like their camp. Although photographs of the Jewish inmates and the interior of Lager Vereinshaus had been strictly forbidden, some old photographs taken by Lichtenauers of the streets just outside the barracks that housed the Jewish women and girls were included in the reunion exhibit.

The women were looking forward to the visit to the site of their former camp. They were both astounded and happy, and extremely pleased the town had erected on school grounds a memorial stone to them.

Blanka Pudler expressed their gratitude in a moving speech. Blanka told those gathered how she had already heard about the memorial stone from camp mates in Hungary and from Dieter Vaupel, when he visited Budapest two months before the meeting. She was very touched and grateful but now that she was in Hessisch Lichtenau, there was a special satisfaction to see that people would be reminded of the suffering of the 1,000 Jewish women right in front of a school. To her, it was so important that young people learn about their fate and the Holocaust so that hatred never rules the world again. She thanked everyone there for remembering them with the memorial stone.

Figure 17: Jewish survivor taking down inscription on Memorial Stone, 1987. Photo by Gregor Espelage.

That day Blanka Pudler also promised that she would come and tell her story to young people in Germany whenever she was wanted.

After the September 1987 meeting, Dieter would arrange for Blanka to speak to students in schools all over Germany. For her efforts with schoolchildren, in 2012 the German government awarded Blanka the Order of Merit of the Federal Republic of Germany.

***

While the site of the camp in town had been rebuilt extensively in recent years, the ruins of the munitions factory remained as they had been when explored by Dieter and his students during Project Week four years earlier.

On a rainy Saturday morning outside the community centre in Hessisch Lichtenau, former German 'duty' workers or those who had been required to work at the factory, forced labourers from France, The Netherlands, Poland and the Soviet Union, and the Hungarian-Jewish women from Lager Vereinshaus, boarded two buses for a tour of their former workplace. In 'Forced laborers visit Hirschhagen; Awakens memories' (7 September 1987), HNA, a reporter wrote, 'Some are afraid of what awaits them there; but the desire to return to the place of suffering again and to work through one's own past is stronger.'

The Hungarian-Jewish women were intimately familiar with the nearly five-kilometer route from Hessisch Lichtenau to the munitions factory. Only 10 minutes by bus, they knew that it took well over an hour by foot, having walked to the factory from the Vereinshaus camp then back again, six days a week, no matter the weather. Sometimes, for unknown reasons, they were marched to the train station in Hessisch Lichtenau to board the train to the Fürstenhagen station, and then walked the rest of the way, another 20 to 40 minutes depending on where they worked in the factory.

What would become apparent to Dieter Vaupel over his years of research and interviewing survivors is that some of the Jewish women and girls had more of a 'tunnel vision' view of the munitions factory as opposed to the other workers. Depending on where they were employed, the Jewish women and girls knew only a small part of the entire factory on the 250-hectare site. They only saw where they worked and were not told about anything else going on in the massive facility. For some, their fragmented memories held stark images of the dark windowless rooms where they worked, and the long underground tunnels that they walked each day to reach them. They had not seen enough of the factory site to accurately place where they had been.

However, one area familiar to some of the Jewish women who attended the 1987 gathering were the loading ramps near the filing station, where they

Figure 18: Luciana Nissim and Martha Frank on bus to munitions factory. Private Archive Dieter Vaupel.

had loaded bombs onto the railway cars. This was the first stop on their munitions factory tour.

After the filing station, the HNA reporter covering the tour of the factory, wrote, 'The next stop after a walk over muddy paths and past barking dogs is the former press in the so-called Carpathanians. Here, too, the former workers begin to talk spontaneously, ask Vaupel for details and have the site plan explained.'

Someone asked if there were not any more buildings at this location. Dieter had brought a copy of the original site map that the students had discovered during Project Week 1983, and he saw the man was right; a building had been torn down. A woman said, 'I recognize these buildings. I worked here.' Dieter explained the production process in the buildings and the importance of the individual buildings. Others began to talk about where they worked in the buildings, how hard the work was, and the dangers they were exposed to.

What struck many of the Jewish women was how different some parts of the munitions factory looked. Dieter told them this was not surprising as the Americans had blown up about a third of the buildings in 1945 as part of their demolition effort, and the extensive camouflage measures in place during the war had been removed.

Still, others were able to recognize individual areas of the vast factory or the section inside the building where they worked. Sometimes someone would experience a sense memory as when Magda Kornfein entered the press building and said it still smelled the same way it did 40 years ago.

Many Project Week students also went along for the munitions factory tour. The Hungarian women were deeply touched by the interest of these young people.

Figure 19: Magda Kornfein in press building explaining her work to Dieter Vaupel, 1987. Private Archive Dieter Vaupel.

Figure 20: Walking tour with survivors and students, Judith Isaacson front left, 1987. Private Archive Dieter Vaupel.

Among the former slave labourers taking part in the walking tour was Judith Isaacson. Judith was the Hungarian-born Jewish survivor who had come from the United States with her husband to visit Hessisch Lichtenau in 1983. As she told Dieter, when she went looking for the underground munitions factory to verify her memories, locals told her that no such place existed. Because of his research, Dieter could now explain why some of the women such as Judith believed they had been in an underground factory.

The women who believed they were in an underground factory were literally 'under ground' but not in the same way as Dora Mittelbau in Thruringia, the well-known underground factory where the Nazis built V-2 missiles.

In Hirschhagen there had not been a massive excavation with construction underground. Instead the Nazi engineers had first built production buildings spread over the 250-hectare site. Then came massive earthen walls that towered over some of the buildings. These earthworks formed mounds over the buildings. Hundreds of trees and shrubbery were planted on the mounds to completely blend into the forest. The Jewish women and girls who worked in these buildings would then have entered through a kind of tunnel in what appeared to be pristine woodland.

So these buildings were more like earth-covered buried bunkers. The misperceptions of the women thinking the tunnel-like entrances were leading them underground came from their very restricted view of the

Figure 21: Tunnel-like entrance to a building in the munitions factory, 2016. Private Archive Dieter Vaupel.

extensively camouflaged factory, and purposely not being told where they were.

The munitions factory in Hirschhagen escaped all aerial bombing during the war. It is unlikely this was due to the camouflage. There were, for example, multi-storey buildings that could not be hidden because of the production process. The elaborate camouflage measures could also not hide the track systems or settling tanks. British aerial photographs taken during the war clearly showed the size and location of the factory.

So why was the munitions factory not bombed? Some speculate that the Allies' explicit strategy was to bomb the civilian population, which was still fanatically behind Hitler, in order to break its morale. Others point to the presence of thousands of foreign forced labourers in Hirschhagen, who would have been caught up in the bombing. A third theory supposes that the munitions factory was not bombed so that after the war the Allies could learn about the advanced manufacturing processes and production technology of the Nazis. Dieter Vaupel favours this latter theory but admits that his research has yet to yield a definitive answer. He fears that the true reasons, like many other details of the Hirschhagen story, are becoming more difficult to learn as they recede further into history.

✳✳✳

The September 1987 reunion would be the last time the ex-workers of the munitions factory would gather in Hessisch Lichtenau, but not the last time the Jewish women and girls of Lager Vereinshaus would be the subject of a student Project Week. These survivors would continue to be honoured by the young people of Hessisch Lichtenau in remarkable and unexpected ways.

12

Book About A Book

More than 35 years after Dieter Vaupel and his students took the first steps to find out what happened in their town during the Nazi regime, their effort still resonated in Hessisch Lichtenau. In recent years even Ingo Geisler, the town's former mayor who once feared that unlocking the past too quickly could hurt the town's reputation, has publicly praised the work of Dieter and the students.

The history of Hessisch Lichtenau during the Nazi era is now an independent teaching topic in the local schools, and the Jewish women and girls of the Vereinshaus camp are an ongoing Project Week subject.

In 2019, Project Week students honoured the Jewish women and girls by organizing a human chain to mark the almost five kilometer path that the inmates walked from the Vereinshaus camp to the munitions factory in Hirschhagen. Almost 2,000 townspeople held hands and formed the chain.

Figure 22: Human chain to honour the women and girls of Lager Vereinshaus, 2019. Photo by ExtraTip Werra-Meißner.

Stefan Reuss, an alumni of Project Week 1987, was among those who took part in the 2019 human chain. Stefan, in his role as the district administrator for Werra-Meißner, the home district to Hessisch Lichtenau, and as chairman of the board of directors of the Kreissparkasse Savings Bank, has unceasingly backed initiatives that support the memory of the Jewish women and girls and forced workers of the munitions factory.

***

In the early autumn of 2019, Dieter Vaupel was part of an event in California that featured talks and a panel discussion on the newly-published biography of Lager Vereinshaus survivor Kati Kellner Salcer and her husband Willi Salcer, *No Past Tense: Love and Survival in the Shadow of the Holocaust*.

The event speakers included Kati's family members and author D.Z. Stone. Holocaust scholar Dr. Holli Levitsky led a panel discussion. Also in attendance was Dr. Michael Berenbaum, founding and former Project Director for the United States Holocaust Memorial Museum and former President and CEO of the Shoah Visual History Foundation, who wrote the Foreword for *No Past Tense*.

Kati Salcer was a Czech Jew who due to the shifting borders was swept up by the Holocaust in Hungary. Kati and other Jewish women and girls from the region were sent to Auschwitz and then to Hessisch Lichtenau. Those from Kati's village of Plesivec included Clara Loebl, Ilona Kellner, Vera Kellner, Ica Moravi, Edith Pincasz, Martha Pincasz, Magda Fisher and Eva Fisher.

Kati and the Fisher sisters were among the so-called 'Canary Girls' whose skin turned yellow from their work in the factory with the chemical trinitrotoluene (TNT). The chemical gravely affected their health. When Kati and Magda found Eva Fisher dead in their barracks, Kati, who spoke German, asked a sympathetic German guard if they could give Eva a proper Jewish burial instead of sending Eva's body to the oven in Auschwitz. The guard said yes, so Kati and Magda were up all night digging a grave for Eva on the grounds of the Vereinshaus camp. Eva was buried by the morning. It is not known if her body was discovered when the camp was cleared and the school built.

The California event, entitled, 'The Never Told Story of the Missing Nazi Labor Camp,' centred on the profound impact that Dieter Vaupel's research in uncovering the history of the munitions factory had for survivors, in particular validating the memories of Kati Kellner Salcer.

For the event, Dieter worked with current Project Week students and a local television station, Open Channel in Kassel, to film a short documentary about the Jewish women and girls.

Figure 23: Alida Scheibli and Dieter Vaupel at reading for documentary. Photo by: Reiner Sander.

Interspersed with a tour of the former munitions factory narrated by Dieter Vaupel, the German high school students re-enacted scenes and read from Blanka Pudler's memoir. An English version of the documentary was shown at the event at the Jewish Community Center in Redondo Beach, California, on 5 December 2019.

Alida Scheibli, who read from Blanka's memoir, said it was a great honour to work on the project but she was quite nervous: 'It's a very serious, but also sensitive topic, so taking a wrong step is not an option. While these events occurred several decades ago, it is undeniable that their shadows still linger to this day, and it felt great to take a stand with this movie and make it abundantly clear that history cannot be allowed to repeat itself.'

Student Rieke Bauer, who played Blanka Pudler in the documentary, says her interest was sparked by Blanka's memoir: 'We – Marilen, Lea, our classmate Clara and I – read the book about Blanka's story shortly after it was published. During a Project Week we presented the book to every class at our school and talked a lot about the fate of Blanka and the other Jewish women and girls.'

The students felt that spending time in the cold forest during filming helped them gain a better grasp of what the Jewish women and girls had

Figure 24: Rieke Bauer as Blanka being marched from camp to the munitions factory. Dieter Vaupel Documentary 2019.

endured. 'We stood outside in the forest for many hours to make the film and felt the cold that Blanka reported. It is something else to feel hands and feet hurt by the cold than to read it in a book while lying comfortably in bed,' said Marilen Schäfer, who played a Jewish slave labourer in the film.

Student Lea Achler played Helga, a young German woman who was required to work in the factory. Whenever she could, Helga would bring small bites of food to Blanka, who could speak German.

Lea agreed with Marilen that filming in the cold gave them a better understanding. 'I was frozen over after four hours of filming and, unlike the Jews at that time, I was still wearing relatively warm clothes.'

Lea also had concerns that most of their fellow students were not aware of what had happened during the Nazi era. She found it 'sad that many young people do not even know what happened in Hessisch Lichtenau…what happened right on their own doorstep is not even known…the National Socialist history of every city should not be forgotten.'

Rieke Bauer thinks young people were not aware of the town's Nazi past because, 'today's generation of students were born after everything around National Socialism, after the fall of the Berlin Wall and have no direct connection to what happened'. Rieke believes it is important that young people learn what happened to not only 'realize what good conditions we live under today and to begin to appreciate this,' but also so 'what happened back then never happens again'.

Alida Scheibli believes:

> Movies like this are undoubtedly necessary reminders of a thankfully bygone era, and prompt us to remember what humanity was capable of in its darkest hours. As is the nature of time, the amount of contemporary witnesses in the world grows thinner by the day. This in combination with improper education about the topic leads to younger generations developing an emotional disconnect to the early 20th century. Some of these people go as far as to joke about these times, due to a lack of understanding; I believe they'd change their mind if they had a chance to see the moments of true agony and despair women had to experience 70 years ago.

For Marilen Schäfer, it is also especially important that 'if you live in a place where women and girls have suffered, you should not let their memory be forgotten'.

***

Over the years Dieter Vaupel stayed in contact with many of the Jewish women sent to Hessisch Lichtenau from Auschwitz. Sometimes he would see them when he was in Budapest or when some returned to Hessisch

Figure 25: Marilen Schäfer and Lea Achler following route of Jewish workers from camp to factory. Dieter Vaupel Documentary 2019.

Lichtenau to visit. Many of the women had developed long-standing friendships with townspeople since staying in their homes during the 1987 reunion.

Dieter would correspond with the women living in Hungary as well as Israel and the United States and other countries. Altogether, he would form friendships and correspondences with over 200 of them. One particularly strong friendship was between Dieter and Blanka Pudler.

When Blanka first came to Hessisch Lichtenau for the 1987 reunion meeting, Dieter immediately recognized her extraordinary communication skills and ability to connect with students. Dieter and Jürgen Jessen arranged for Blanka to speak in schools in Germany and after returning to Budapest, she would also speak in schools in Hungary. Blanka continued speaking in schools as long as her health permitted. In 2014 she made her last visit to Germany to speak to students.

Dieter also encouraged Blanka to write her memoir, but she was not a natural writer and found the task daunting. She asked if perhaps Dieter would help her get her thoughts written down. After much discussion they agreed to proceed. They worked together on the memoir on and off for years.

Unfortunately, Blanka's memoir was not yet completed before she died in 2017. Speaking at her funeral, Dieter promised that he would not let Blanka Pudler's story be lost; he would finish her memoir for her. A German version of her memoir, *On a Strange Uninhabitable Planet*, was published in 2018.

In 2020, the British Publisher Vallentine Mitchell decided to publish Blanka Pudlers's memoir in English. Specializing in books of Jewish, Middle Eastern and Holocaust studies, among Vallentine Mitchell's first publications was Anne Frank's Diary. Vallentine Mitchell also asked that a 'book about the book' that detailed Dieter Vaupel and his students' efforts to unmask what happened in their town be included with Blanka's memoir. This is that book.

Afterword
Not a Dream

After the war, whenever Kati Kellner Salcer described being sent from Auschwitz to a small labour camp in Lichtenau, Germany, to work in an underground factory that had thousands of forced workers, she was not quite believed, even by her husband. How could it be, her engineer husband wondered, that there could be a pristine forest on top of an underground factory with thousands of workers? And why has no one heard of this place? Perhaps, he suggested, it was a dream from a traumatized memory. Kati, after all, was only a 16-year-old girl who had just lost her mother, brother and grandmother in Auschwitz.

So Kati stopped talking about her wartime experiences until 1999, when her son enlisted a writer so he could learn what his parents experienced during the war. I am that writer.

When I tried to locate where Kati had been sent, I quickly learned there were many places in Germany called 'Lichtenau'. Even if I had known it was 'Hessisch Lichtenau', and had been lucky enough to come across the book on its 700 years of history published by the city in 1990, I still would have found no mention of the munitions factory and the camps. Gregor Espelage and Dieter Vaupel, with the support of the History Workshop, did publish a supplementary booklet that closed this gap in the historical record. But neither of these documents were very accessible in 1999 to a writer in the United States (who did not read German), especially given the limitations at the time of the internet as a research tool and the few libraries that had searchable electronic databases.

Still, Kati's story was so vivid and unchanging that I became convinced that she must have been working in some kind of underground site. I asked a geology professor friend, Dr. William Menke at Columbia University, if he knew of some natural formation or mine in Germany that might have been used during the war. He said he would look into it and mentioned it to his wife, Dr. Dallas Abbott, also a geologist.

Dallas told me that Kati's experience sounded very familiar to her. It was the same wartime story that she had heard from Judith Isaacson, her next-door neighbour while growing up in Maine. Dallas gave me a copy of Judith's memoir, *Seed of Sarah: Memoir of a Survivor*. There it was, the labour camp and the underground factory. Amazingly, my friend's childhood neighbour had been in the same forced labour camp as Kati Kellner Salcer.

When I spoke with Judith, she recounted her 1983 visit to Hessisch Lichtenau, and being told there had been no underground munitions factory. It was only a few years later when she received in the mail a scholarly paper by a German history teacher named Dieter Vaupel that her memory was verified.

Judith put me in contact with Dieter, who confirmed that Kati had been among those sent from Auschwitz to become slave workers in a massive munitions factory. And yes, she and the others had entered the factory through a tunnel-like entrance in a dense forest, and had been working 'underground'. However I would later learn not as deep underground as the entrances and camouflage led Kati and others to believe.

From Judith Isaacson I first learned that Dieter Vaupel had faced resistance, even threats, for his research that unlocked this history. I was also impressed that the research had begun as a project by his high school students. I asked why he persisted after being threatened. He responded in a one-line email: 'It was the right thing to do.'

Being able to tell Kati Salcer that she had not imagined this place, that she had been there and had not dreamed it, was one of the most satisfying moments of my life.

When Blanka Pudler spoke at the ceremony for the memorial stone in 1987, she talked about how important Dieter's work had been for her life. She recounted her reaction when she first received a copy of Dieter's book about the Jewish women and girls of the Vereinshaus camp.

She took the book from the mailbox, opened the envelope, and when she saw it was about where she had been, she began to immediately read. She remained pinned to the spot by her post box until she finished the entire book.

Blanka was shocked to see all the facts and figures about her own experience in black and white. To her as well, everything had seemed like it was just a bad dream. Now she had the evidence. It was real. Like Kati Salcer and Judith Isaacson, Blanka Pudler had not imagined any of it. This had happened to them.

D.Z. Stone

PART II

How a 15 Year-Old Girl Survived Auschwitz and Slave Labour

Foreword
Blanka's Story Should Not Get Lost

I met Blanka Pudler a good three decades ago, during my search for survivors of the former SS concentration subcamp Hessisch Lichtenau. During my first visit to Budapest – followed by many more – I felt that she was a particularly warm and caring woman.

My last visit to the Hungarian capital was in 2017, when I paid my respects to Blanka during her funeral at the Budapest Jewish Cemetery. I addressed Blanka's family and mourners with these heartfelt words:

I am tremendously sad about Blanka's death. The first time we met in Budapest in 1986 was when I was busy with my scientific research about the forced labourers in the ammunition factory of Hessisch Lichtenau. Blanka was one of the thousand slave workers there. My first meeting with Blanka was the beginning of a wonderful, deep friendship for the next 31 years until the present day.'

Blanka was in our country many times. She spoke to thousands of students in the schools of our region. The teenagers were shocked about her bad fate, but they were also impressed by this warm-hearted woman. After all these terrible experiences in Auschwitz and Hessisch Lichtenau she came to Germany without bitterness, she came as a friend.

At one of her lectures, she said to the students: 'I have decided to continue this work as long as I am asked and my strength is sufficient to enable the present generation to learn from our cruel past and to build a beautiful, more just future for themselves.'

I want to say thank you, Blanka, for everything you have done for us. We have lost not only a wonderful, empathic friend, but also one of the last contemporary witnesses who could report on Auschwitz and the atrocities of the Nazis. Many people in Germany who had the chance to get to know you will miss you. Especially me. Blanka, you will live on in our hearts."

During our years of friendship Blanka Pudler and I had countless conversations. I am grateful that I got to know and understand her better and better. Almost 15 years ago I had the idea to write down her moving story, which she had told so often in front of young people in Germany.

I told Blanka that I wanted to make a book out of it, a very personal and emotional book, not just a factual documentation, and she agreed immediately. So I went to work to find a literary language for Blanka that was similar to her lectures. I wanted a language that young people, but also interested adults, could immerse themselves in and feel Blanka's world of that time. After the first pages were written, I gave them to Blanka. We talked about what had or had not expressed something in the same way she had experienced it. As I continued to write and work with Blanka's feedback, I was able to find the right tone, the right language. We settled on the first-person perspective of 15-year-old Blanka so the reader could experience her thoughts and feelings.

Unfortunately, my own career kept me from completing Blanka's book. After Blanka's death I told myself that since she could no longer speak for herself that I had to speak for her now. I had to finish the story of her life and suffering. I had to complete the book she had started with me so that her story would be preserved for future generations.

That was what I promised to Blanka Pudler and myself on the day of her funeral in Budapest. Her story should not and could not be lost.

Figure 26: Blanka Pudler in 2008 in Hessisch Lichtenau at the memorial stone that was placed on the former camp grounds in 1986.

13

Why Are You Lying?

Suddenly the SS women are standing in our barracks. A Polish block elder accompanies them. What on earth is that supposed to mean? During the few days I've been in Auschwitz I have already experienced that one has to be careful. They are up to no good that's for sure. We, the girls and women are all looking cautiously at each other. We are all insecure. We can't find answers to the questions that are going through our minds. Neither in the faces of the others. What do they want from us? All of a sudden it became quiet in our barracks. Dead quiet. You never know what will happen next. Insecurity lies over us just like a dark cloud. What's coming next? We don't know, we're afraid. Can it get any worse for us? Predictability and knowing what is to come next seems to be something from another world, a world to which we no longer belong. In this place, it does no longer apply. Like almost everything else. Everything important in our lives before has been erased. Who are we now? Are we even human anymore?

The robotic voice of an SS woman tears me from my thoughts. 'Which of you has not yet reached the age of 16?' I hear one of the guards asking. Once again we cast uncertain glances at each other. 'This concerns me', flashes through my mind. Just a few more weeks, then I'm supposed to turn 15. My heart is pounding. I can hear the thumping in my temples and I can't think straight. Why are they asking this question now? But before I can think about it any further, her postscript gives me an incredible joy: 'Because they can go to their mother!'

This is what I have been longing for almost every minute since I was taken here. To this strange place where I don't understand so many things. My mother! I will see her again! So the rumours about all the terrible things happening here are not true after all! I wouldn't and couldn't believe it. Nobody really speaks openly about it, but I notice from so many reactions, from the sadness that is constant, from the resignation: all our family members and friends who were separated from us when we arrived, many of my fellow prisoners have long since given up. There are rumours. It is said that hundreds, even thousands of new arrivals are killed here every day. I cannot imagine that. How could such a thing be possible? Thousands killed every day? We are not treated like human beings here, that's what I realized from the very first moment. But it seems absurd. There's no reason to kill us. What have we done? And why did they let us live? None of this makes any sense to me.

And now these words of the SS woman: 'Because those can go to their mother!' All these negative rumours are obviously false. My mother's alive! I'm sure she longs for me as much as I do for her. It seems to be true what they promised us when we arrived, when I was torn away from my mother by force and in tears. 'You will see her again!' the uniformed men had shouted to me as I wouldn't let go of her. They smiled strangely, but I wanted to believe them. Now what these men promised will come true.

Since I am not even 15 years old, I answer without a moment's hesitation: 'I, I want to go to my mother', I hear myself saying in a calm voice. My heart jumps for joy anticipating the reunion with my beloved mother. I have her image in my mind and I can already feel her warmth, I can smell and feel her. Soon I will have her back and feel this feeling of security of my childhood again. Nothing can happen to me when I am with my mother! Her love has carried me through my whole childhood.

As a farewell I hug my big sister Aranka, who is almost as close to me as my mother. Sure, I did have a fight with my sister during our childhood days. But when it came down to it, we were always there for each other. Our relationship is very special. Much closer than with our other siblings. I look Aranka in the eyes and feel how hard it is for her to say goodbye to me. Only a few days ago we found each other by chance in the huge crowds of the camp. I had almost given up hope of finding her. Aranka notices by now how hard it is for me to say goodbye too, she sees how my eyes fill with tears. She detaches herself from my gaze and says in a strong voice to comfort me: 'You go to mama, I'm old enough to manage on my own for now! We'll get back together later.'

Full of emotion at this farewell scene and with a warm-hearted look that has become rare in this place, the block elder standing next to the SS women looks at us. Then she suddenly changes her expression, gets a hardness in her face that I don't understand. She comes up to me and says loudly in a stern voice that seems to tolerate no contradiction: 'Why are you lying? I know that you are already older than 16! You mustn't lie here!' What does that mean? How can I relate this to the change in her gaze? What is she doing? She was so honest in her pity that I can't understand anything at first. I should now best rely on my feelings.

The SS woman in command here now turns her attention to me and asks in a sharp tone: 'So what is the truth? Are you over 16 or not?' Loud and reproachful, these words come to my ear, hammer into my brain. 'What is the truth? What is the truth?' What should I answer? From my sister, whom

I look at from the corners of my eye, I can't expect any help in this situation. I must react immediately not to arouse suspicion or even draw the wrath of these unpredictable SS women on me. So, without thinking about it, I rely on my feelings and instinctively answer: 'Yes, I will even be 17 soon!' 'Then why are you lying, bitch?' I hear the SS woman say in an even sharper voice. 'We'll get rid of that here! Don't try that again!' Two slaps on the face like I've never had before in my life. Right – left. Clap – clap. My skull is pounding, I'm tumbling, then I'm pushed in the direction of my sister by this woman, who suddenly appears to be a vicious monster in my eyes of a child. Aranka cannot react fast enough to at least try to catch me. So that I hit the barrack floor next to her hard.

Much later do I learn that these slaps, the screaming and the hard push are trifles compared to what I would have expected if I had remained honest concerning my true age: my life was saved at that moment! For some reason, which I don't know, the block elder, from whom I actually had nothing good to expect, took pity on me. A human emotion in an inhuman situation. She is obviously not yet as indifferent as many others. At least not in this moment. Maybe, as I think later, she saw how hard it was for me to say goodbye to my sister. Perhaps she herself once went through a similar situation, which did not end as well as in my case. Maybe she simply wanted to save a child who had touched her heart. At least one of the many that could not be saved.

All the girls who came forward that day were actually sent to their mothers: directly to the gas chambers of Auschwitz, where their mothers, just like my beloved mother, were mercilessly driven and murdered. Instead of the promised water, the deadly gas Zyklon B came out of the showers. None of the girls who left our barracks that day to go to their mothers was ever seen again. The rumours of what actually happened to them and countless others are spreading, becoming so dense that I too am losing faith in a miracle.

In any case, from that day on, when the SS women appeared in our barracks and the Polish woman, a stranger to me, courageously intervened, the relationship with my six years older sister Aranka became even more intimate than before. Although Aranka can give me a lot of security whenever she is near me, after the event I live in constant fear of being separated from her and then being left alone. All alone.

Now I have really arrived in this dark, demonic world of Auschwitz-Birkenau. Without a thought that it might not be so bad after all. Without hope. I have arrived in Birkenau, hell on earth. A place where you lose all illusions. A place of degradation and dehumanization. So this is where my 'life' will take place! I cannot believe or understand all the things I have to experience here every day. It is surreal. What happened that they brought me here? In my childish mind, I can't put all of this together. Where am I? An unknown feeling comes over me. I feel strange, lonely and without any perspective. For me, here it's like being on a strange planet that's actually completely uninhabitable. Everything that I encounter here has nothing, absolutely nothing, more to do with what I and all of us previously understood by 'life'.

14

___

Childhood: Poverty Always
Caught Up with Us

For us – my parents, my two sisters, my brother and I – it had never been easy. I was born in 1929 in Aknaszlatina, a small town in the Carpathian Ukraine, close to the Romanian border. At that time I was named Blanka Adler. The idyllic little town on the small river Tisza has had a very eventful history due to its border location. The town is especially known for its salt deposits and its salty springs.

I was a real 'nestling', a late arrival in our family, which was actually complete before I was born. My siblings had a distance of several years to me. Roszi, the oldest, was already nine, Dezső eight and Aranka six years old at my birth. My mother Eszter and my father Mathias were both deeply religious and followed the rules that Judaism imposed on them. The area of Aknaszlatina was an area where many Jews lived. My parents talked in Yiddish. Of course, the Sabbath was kept in our family, and my father regularly attended the synagogue. In other respects, too, faith had a firm place in our everyday life, not only on the high holidays. So I was brought up in the Jewish faith and Jewish tradition.

Poverty marked my life and the lives of all of us from the very first day. Again and again in later years of life I was confronted with people who thought: 'All Jews are rich!' Prejudices that had been carried on for centuries and then led the National Socialists to exclude Jews from social life in a perfidious way, and finally to murder them systematically. 'The rich, greedy Jews who only want to suck the blood of others are our enemies, are to blame for all the evils of the world and must therefore be exterminated!' This was hammered into the Reichsdeutsche Volksgemeinschaft. And we Jews became enemies of the people.

Sure, there were and are many wealthy Jews, many who have become wealthy in trade and banking. This has historical reasons. Due to occupational restrictions in the cities of the Middle Ages, it was not possible for Jews to learn a so-called 'honest' trade. The guilds did not allow this, excluded the Jews. So they had to look for other ways to earn a living. Many specialized in trade, others became moneylenders, which was denied to

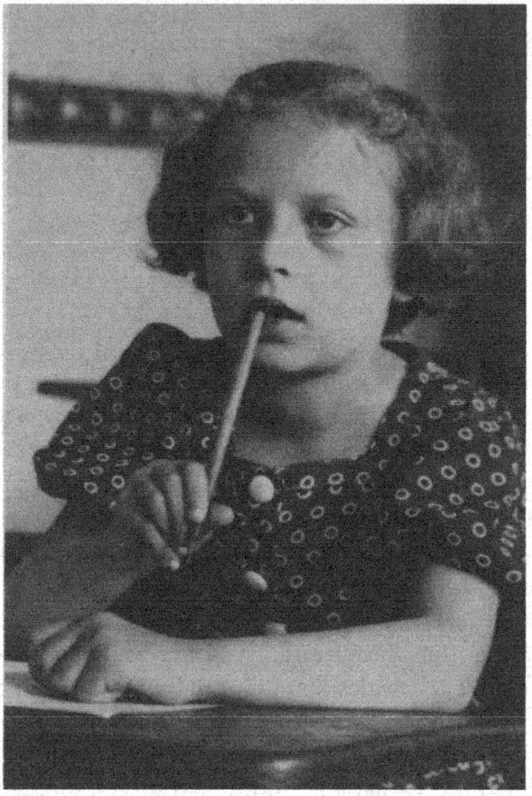

Figure 27: Blanka as a pupil in the German primary school in Käsmark. Private Estate Blanka Pudler.

Christians at that time. These were reasons why many Jews came into money. Money transactions and trade were practically forced upon them and they had to accept this role.

But we were far away from wealth in Aknaszlatina, this had nothing to do with our living situation. I had not been born on the sunny side of life. My father was neither a banker nor a rich merchant. He struggled with his work as a men's tailor, but always had too little to do to be able to feed his family of six. My mother, who lovingly cared for us children, often did not know in the morning when she got up what to give us for lunch. We literally lived from hand to mouth.

In hope of new and more orders for my father and better living conditions, we left Aknaszlatina and moved for the first time in 1930, my second year of life. Our destination was Käsmark, a place below the High Tatras. We moved to a region that was German speaking at that time. So I learned German practically as my 'mother tongue', went to the German kindergarten and then to the German school. At home, within our family, German was now spoken and Yiddish was still spoken. I was a good student, went to school full of enthusiasm and literally absorbed everything that was offered to me there. I learned to write, read and calculate quickly and without any problems, which opened up a whole new world for me. My interest in all the new things that were offered to me at school was great, many things were incredibly exciting for me.

It was a happy time in Käsmark for me as a child, the worries and hardships of my parents, my father's struggle for work and economic survival – I didn't really understand all that at the age I was a primary school student. It was only later that I realized the hardship we must have been in.

Figure 28: The only photograph Blanka kept of her family: 1932 in Käsmark Blanka sitting between her parents Mathias and Eszter Adler, maiden name Pollak, behind her from left Dezsö, Roszi and Aranka. Private Estate Blanka Pudler.

Käsmark was almost 400 kilometers from Aknaszlatina. The reason for our move to such a distant place was the poor living and working conditions. An uncle had advised my father to move. He told him that there was a lot of good work for him as a tailor in Käsmark, because he could sew ski suits. However, our life of privation did not improve in Käsmark during this time. On the contrary, we were even worse off, the orders we had hoped for did not come, and my father was unable to pay his taxes. So his business was seized by the authorities. Even the fabrics that did not belong to us but to the customers were taken away from him.

Once again we moved in 1937 still carrying the hope in our hearts that the situation would change for the better. We came to the town of Leva, 200 kilometers to the west, which today belongs to Slovakia. This time with another idea in our pocket: my father had a very beautiful voice and he dreamed of becoming a cantor in the synagogue. He had relations with a rabbi in Leva and he promised him that he could get a cantor position there. My poor father always hoped to find a better job somewhere, but unfortunately poverty always followed us. The cantor's position didn't work out and my father had to go back to the sewing machine.

Nevertheless he never gave up hope. He was not allowed to lose it. He had us, his four children and his wife, whom he had to support somehow. He struggled, he did not surrender to his fate, hoping again and again to earn more somewhere else and thereby giving us a better life. It could not have been due to his diligence, he struggled from morning to night, just like my mother who lovingly cared for us.

Leva is a small town in the Slovakian uplands. Both Slovakian and Hungarian were spoken there. Both languages were completely unknown to me, so that I had enormous difficulties, because at school the lessons were held in Slovakian, I did not understand anything at first. In addition, I was mocked and laughed at by the other children because of my lack of language skills. This was very embarrassing, caused me great grief as a child and completely robbed me of my self-esteem. My eagerness to learn was slowed down at first, but my ambition came back after a while: I wanted to master this new language at all costs.

In autumn 1938, the area where we lived fell to Hungary as a result of an agreement with Nazi Germany. The language at school was now changed to Hungarian, and once again I understood nothing. I had to continue the fourth primary school class, which I had started in Slovakian, now in Hungarian. But only for a short time – as it soon turned out. Since we did not have Hungarian citizenship, we were immediately deported to my birthplace, Aknaszlatina, 600 kilometers further east, as unwanted foreigners. How my parents were able to cope with these constant moves and the great distances in between, with us four children and in view of their poverty, will always remain a mystery to me. A sister of my mother got us a small apartment in Aknaszlatina. We packed our few things together in Leva and returned to our old home by bus.

When we arrived in Aknaszlatina nothing was the same as eight years before. The political conditions had changed radically. Now the Ukrainian nationalists ruled there. Only schools where Ukrainian was the language of instruction were allowed. For me this again meant massive language problems. And all this still in my primary school days. I had just started to learn Slovakian with terrible efforts, now I had to continue school in Ukrainian. And all this without even understanding the language or being able to write the Cyrillic characters. I truly understood almost nothing at school! However, the return to Aknaszlatina had one advantage for me: In this border area to Hungary I was at least able to learn some Hungarian, which would later become very important for me.

Our time in Aknaszlatina was again influenced by political changes, which meant that we all had to move again. We had not been able to put down roots anywhere. In May 1939 our village was annexed to Hungary together with the Transylvanian territories. This enabled us to return to Leva, where we had been deported as illegal foreigners only a few months earlier. I was now able to finish the fourth grade of primary school in Hungarian. I

Figure 29: Blankas' class at the State Middle School in Leva in June 1943, one year before her deportation to Auschwitz. Blanka in the back row, sixth from the right. In the centre of the front row is her beloved class teacher Maria Kovacs, next to her the headmaster. Private Estate Blanka Pudler.

became such a good student that I was even awarded a cash prize at the end of the school year. My mother bought me a sailor's dress, which I had wanted so much. From my own money – otherwise we could never have afforded it. I was so proud of it!

Here, in Leva, I was finally able to find a home together with my siblings and my parents. We spent the next five years there, but it didn't change our social situation much. Our family gradually diminished which at least reduced the economic worries a little. My oldest sister Roszi had got engaged in the meantime and had moved to Budapest to live with her future husband. She wanted to stand on her own feet, looked for a job in Budapest and thus was no longer a burden to my parents. My brother Dezsö had to leave home involuntarily. In 1942 he was drafted into the labour service of the Hungarian army.

Much later I learned that he was in danger of death there almost every day. The Jewish young men who were forced to do this service had to clear the area ahead of the frontline from mines. They were also used in road construction work or other mostly dangerous or physically very strenuous jobs.

Even though only four of us were left and our father only had four mouths to feed, we were and remained a poor Jewish family. Our situation was made worse by the fact that the Jewish population was subjected to more and more restrictions by anti-Jewish laws, which made it even more difficult for my father to get orders. As a Jew, the new laws had deprived him of his licence to practise the tailoring trade. Thus he could only pursue his profession in secret and was practically forced to work on the black market. But it was to get much worse...

15

Only Our Dog Muri Felt Sympathy

Mischief was looming when the Germans succeeded in occupying all strategically important points in Hungary on 19 March 1944, and on 22 March they succeeded in imposing a government acceptable to them. As a 14-year-old I did not notice much of this in the first few days. My older sister Aranka already had her eyes open for her 20 years. But she tried not to burden me with it. When I asked her time and time again: 'Aranka, tell me what's going on, everyone is so strange,' she would only say: 'There's a new government, which worries some people. But you'll see, everything will be fine, don't worry.'

I could tell from my parents that something was wrong. I could feel how insecure they were, how afraid they were. The reason for this was the intensification of anti-Jewish laws. The weeks in March and April were unbearable, my parents tried to ensure normality in everyday life, but everything was now even more difficult, even more tiring for them. My father was practically unemployed, because moonlighting became even more dangerous for him. What was to become of us?

At school I felt a strange atmosphere, which gradually increased. In our class at the Bürgerschule we were the only two Jewish children. I noticed that some classmates avoided contact with me and Magda, the other Jewish girl. They wanted no longer to deal with us. My German teacher was openly anti-Semitic and I could not avoid being constantly mistreated in front of the others. I had to bear being humiliated.

At the beginning of April we all had to finish the Bürgerschule with the fourth grade, because the school building was converted into German barracks without further ado. At our graduation ceremony I was forced to wear the yellow Star of David on my beautiful festive dress for the first time. Even though the background only gradually became clear to me, I felt the immense humiliation that was connected with this public identification as a Jew. Fortunately I had a very empathetic and courageous class teacher: On her responsibility we were allowed to take off the yellow star at the celebration.

From now on Jews had to walk around with this star on their clothes wherever they went. We now had the duty to wear the Jewish star in public.

In addition there were curfews and shopping prohibitions and the fear of assaults. I felt excluded, stigmatized. What had I done to be treated like this? We spoke little about it in our family, depressed we accepted this change in our life, but we tried not to completely lose our courage to live. We were already experienced in this.

The events became increasingly worse in a short time, the situation becaming more severe for us. At the beginning of May all Jews from the area around our town were taken to Leva by force. A ghetto was set up to which all Jews from Leva were brought in mid-May. The conditions in the ghetto were absolutely inhumane: penned together, no adequate facilities for hygiene, no toilets, hardly any water, and there was almost nothing to eat.

Initially we were lucky and were able to stay in our little house under guard of the Hungarian gendarmerie. We lived there in a very confined space together with two other Jewish families. The little daughter of one of the families had suffered from scarlet fever and they wanted to avoid an epidemic, so at first they did not force us to go into the ghetto. But soon that was over too.

The next disaster, one which was going to change everything that had been important to us, was already approaching. I will never forget it – it was on a Friday afternoon. We were preparing for Sabbath. The Sabbath cake was in the oven, the whole house smelled good and we were looking forward to the cake. Suddenly German SS men, accompanied by Hungarian gendarmes, invaded our apartment and chased us out of the house. We had barely a minute to gather our things together to take some of the little we had. In our haste we packed everything we could get a hold of into a knotted sheet instead of a suitcase.

When my father wanted to return to the house to fetch his prayer shawl, which he had forgotten in the hurry, and which was of special importance to him as a believing Jew, the SS men threw it to the ground and then chased it around the entire yard with heavy foot kicks. My poor father, I could hardly bear to watch! I covered my face with my hands, could not bear the torture. 'Why, why, why?' it went through my mind. Who were those people who did that to my father? Did they have no heart, no pity? Tears stood in my eyes, tears of anger against the men who tormented him and tears of pity for my father, who had had a hard enough life as it was. And now this as well! But all this was only a foretaste of what was to come.

Finally we were all driven onto a waiting truck and transported to the ghetto to join the other Jews. But what should become of Muri, our dog, whom we all loved so much? I heard him barking and whimpering as we were put onto the truck. The SS people pushed him aside with kicks. When we left, I saw him running after the truck. He understood less than I did what was happening here. Our poor dog ran after us until he was completely exhausted and could no longer keep up with the speed of the truck. The poorest one had to stay behind alone. 'Was he the only being in the world who had sympathy for us at the moment?' I asked myself. And yet I also felt pity for him, my beloved Muri. Later, when I remembered our dog, I thought that his fate was certainly still better than what we were to experience. I wish I could have stayed behind too.

In the Leva Ghetto, we were crammed into a very small space. The meagre food was assigned to us. As I learned later, the Hungarian government had reduced the food rations to 100 grams of bread and two cups of soup per person per day. It assumed that the Jews imprisoned in the ghettos would not stay in Hungary much longer anyway. A Sonderkommando under the leadership of Adolf Eichmann had long been preparing the deportation of hundreds of thousands of Jews from the Hungarian ghettos to Auschwitz.

Daily harassment and arbitrary measures marked the days in the ghetto. SS and gendarmes yelled terribly, I was not able to grasp all this. Since I was a shy and frightened young girl anyway, I always sought the closeness of my mother or my big sister Aranka in such situations. At least that gave me a little more security. Several times a day our guards threatened to shoot us all if we did not hand over the hidden gold and jewellery. Gold and jewellery? For the four of us, these were things we might have dreamed of owning one day. But in our poor reality, gold and jewellery had never played a role before. And this was true for most of the Jews from Leva and the surrounding area who were imprisoned with us.

16

Deportation to Auschwitz

On 15 June we were rushed to the train station carrying our luggage accompanied by screams and beatings from SS men and gendarmes. We only had very few belongings anyway, but on the way we had to leave some of them behind, because they were too heavy to carry. With a heavy heart we let it go. The only important thing was that we, my father, my mother, Aranka and I could stay together. I took my mother's hand and squeezed it tight as if I never wanted to let go of it again. The people on the street eagerly took the things that we and the other Jews of Levi had left on the way to the train station. We had the impression that many Levite citizens who were watching us along the street took great pleasure in the way we were treated. Obviously they were just waiting for us not to be able to carry our luggage and for it to become their prey.

When we arrived at the train station, cattle cars with the inscription 'Deutsche Arbeiterumsiedler' (German Worker Relocations) were waiting for us. Cattle cars? That's where we were supposed to go? We soon realized that this was the plan of the SS men. We were no longer being treated humanely during the last weeks. So why not use cattle cars to transport us? We were ordered to enter the wagons, and those who were not fast enough were pushed, kicked and beaten. Everything was swarming with people trying to at least keep their loved ones close to them.

Between 80 and 120 people were penned into each wagon. Fortunately I managed to get into the wagon together with my mother and father. But where had Aranka gone? Suddenly we had lost her within this mess. But then I saw her trying to get into our wagon as one of the last ones. But they wouldn't let her in because there were already too many people inside. She was brutally rejected, no regard was paid to family relations here! She was forced into the next available wagon. We had lost her, but for how long? I shouted after her: 'Aranka, Aranka! We are here, come on!' But she was driven away, she had no chance to fight back. I hoped so much that somehow I'd be able to be near her again soon. We didn't know how long the train ride would take or where they were taking us. Aranka couldn't say goodbye to me nor to our parents. When would we see each other again? Everything had suddenly become so uncertain. Our fate would be decided by others...Nothing was in our hands anymore.

We were given a bucket of drinking water for the 'journey' and another bucket, which was to serve as a 'toilet', was placed in the wagon. The door was locked and all of a sudden it was almost dark, although it was still very bright outside. Only through a few small window slits, which were placed quite high up in the wagon, some daylight fell. When they locked us in, everyone stayed very calm, and after a short discussion we decided to build rows of seats with our luggage and then sit back to back so that everyone would have the same space. There was no room to lie down anyway, there were too many people crammed together in this confinement. The train started with a terrible jolt and we were all thrown on top of each other. Calmly we took our places again.

Figure 30: Deportation of Jews to Auschwitz in Reichsbahn cattle cars where 80 to 100 people were crammed into one car. Archive Auschwitz-Birkenau.

We all had some food with us, but almost nothing to drink. The only ventilation consisted of the two extremely small barred windows. Oxygen deficiency and thirst tormented us terribly during the three-day trip. None of us had expected that the transport would take so long. Of course, everyone was worried about where we might be going after all. Many speculations circulated, but nobody had a conclusive explanation. We all just hoped to reach our final destination.

Everyone could only take a sip of water from the water bucket once a day, and that in the heat of June. After a short time the heat, the dirt and the stench in our wagon had become unbearable. The bucket, which served as a 'toilet', overflowed after only a short time and we had no possibility to empty it. Now I had to relieve myself beside the bucket. I was so ashamed to have to do this in front of everyone. But I was not alone with these feelings. The most important thing was that my father and mother were near me. It was essential that I would not lose them. My mother was crying again and again during the entire journey. She was so desperate. I caressed her face and hands and stayed close to her. My father tried to keep calm, trying not to let his desperation show, but the longer the journey lasted, the more speechless he seemed to be.

People increasingly began to fight, and more and more lost their self-control. Men and women screamed and moaned in confusion, many children and adults cried. Some people fainted, became unconscious, others had nervous breakdowns, still others sat on the floor completely apathetic. Even some people died during the three-day journey in our wagon. The dead simply had to lie between us. Thank God my father remained calm and my mother seemed to recover. At least she did not show her despair anymore. This had a positive effect on me, of course. Without her I would hardly have survived those terrible days in the wagon.

After three days the train suddenly stopped. 'At last,' we all thought. We heard shouting and a strange noise from outside. The door of the wagon was opened and we saw the station sign. 'Auschwitz' was written on it. A place name we had never heard before. We had no idea where we were, but all signs indicated that it was a prison or a guarded camp. Prisoners in striped clothing and uniformed Germans – as we learned later, all of them SS-members – started to tamper with us. They tore and dragged us brutally in a great haste out of the wagons and down onto the ramp, regardless of the fact that we were hardly able to move after the long train ride and being locked up in the narrow wagon. The little we had left of our 'possessions' we had to leave behind inside the wagon.

17

All Alone

'Where is my sister?' was my first thought when I left the wagon. My parents and I searched desperately for her in the large crowd, but in vain. Wherever we looked, we could not find her. We comforted each other with the thought that there would be other chances to find her again. Secretly, however, I had already lost hope in regard to the masses of people on the platform. How – among all these thousands – should this be possible?

We didn't have much time anyway to look around and think about it. The SS men separated us women from the men who had been with us in the wagons with lightning speed, beating us and shouting 'Go, go!' Women and men were lined up separately in rows of five under the barbaric yelling of the guards. Suddenly my father was no longer at our side. Together with my mother, I looked out for him, but we could not spot him. He was simply gone,

Figure 31: Arrival in Auschwitz after a three-day journey in the cattle car. Aranka Adler was among those photographed in front of the carriages. She can be seen on the left-hand side of the photo wearing a headscarf between mothers with children. Archive Auschwitz-Birkenau.

Figure 32: Selection at the ramp in Auschwitz. Archive Yad Vashem.

swallowed up by the anonymous mass. He had become part of it, absorbed by it. Mom and I never even got to say goodbye to him! No last word, no last look, no hug. After the loss of Aranka on the platform at our departure in Leva I didn't have my father with me anymore either. But as a 14-year-old girl, I still had my mom left and I clung to her the closest I could, so that I wouldn't lose her in all the turmoil.

We, the women approached the camp entrance, where several SS soldiers were standing, led by an elegant SS officer in white gloves. As it later turned out, this was SS doctor Dr. Josef Mengele, who became infamously known for abusing Jews, especially twin children, for cruel human experiments. With a wink of his index finger he sent my mother to the left and me to the right in a split second.

Oh no, for god's sake! I don't want to lose her. We can't be separated! Without paying attention to the officers I followed my mother. She was my last resort, my salvation, my heart and my soul. Without her I couldn't survive here. What was I supposed to do if I'd lose her? A soldier who realized I was following my mother made a move trying to hit my head with a nightstick but I was able to dodge. As soon as I did he was ready for a second swing. My mother who saw everything was so frightened I might be hurt and screamed: 'Blanka, go, please go we will meet later again for sure!"

It was the last sentence I've ever heard from her. I never saw my beloved mother again. After a while I was told that the wink to the left at the selection meant immediate death for all who were sent to this site. Older women and children – who were considered no longer or not yet capable for work – were killed immediately in the gas chambers. Today I know that in the summer of 1944 alone, almost 400,000 Hungarian Jews were sent to death upon arrival. The remainder, less than 20 per cent, were to be used for slave labour in German industry. A meticulous record was kept of every single transport that arrived in Auschwitz – on average 3,000 Jews. However, only the number of those who survived the selection and were then sent to the camp was recorded. In addition, the calendar of the concentration camp states 'The others were gassed.'

So after I had had no chance to follow my mother, I had no other choice but to turn to the right. I kept watching my mother, until she disappeared among the other women. Tears rushed into my eyes. I cried bitterly. I was alone. All alone in a strange, threatening world, where I had no clue what was to come. What was waiting for me next?

In that moment of deep mourning a little hope arose within me to at least find my sister. She had to be here somewhere. The moment I lost my mother, I began to look for my sister again. But how was I ever supposed to find her within the huge crowd of humans?

Rows of five were formed and we were chased into a hall. There we were ordered to strip completely naked immediately. It was incredible! Completely surreal! I couldn't grasp what was happening. What were they going to do with us? I had not even shown myself naked to my sister, not to mention my parents. And now I was suddenly forced to undress here in front of all these strangers? I was so ashamed, but like all the others I did what we were told. What would happen next? We were told to remember where we had put our clothes so that we could find them again later. After I had stood there completely naked for a while with my hands crossed in front of my chest, we were ordered to go to another hall.

Women and men in striped clothing and also SS men grabbed and brutally attacked us. They came with scissors and razors, cutting off all our hair except for a few stubble remains. Then they shaved our heads, armpits and pubic hair. A degrading procedure that I let pass completely apathetic upon myself like in a bad nightmare. My brain had simply switched off, otherwise I couldn't have endured it. I no longer perceived the creatures who were doing this to me as humans. They had to be remote-controlled robots.

But that wasn't enough. Obviously, our dignity was to be completely broken, we were no longer to consider ourselves human. We had to take showers afterwards like on a treadmill. Our joy about the fresh water did not last long. The robots rushed back again and sprayed an extraordinarily painful, terribly burning disinfectant, on our heads and armpits, as wet as we were. In the end, we were forced to bend down deep so that we could also have a load of the disinfectant injected into our genital area. All this was deeply humiliating especially for me as a 14-year-old girl. In a flash of time, we were no longer the same people who had arrived in Auschwitz.

The only personal things we had left – our clothes, which we were supposed to take off properly before this special treatment – we could no longer find. Only our shoes were returned to us. With wet bodies we had to line up in rows of five again and wait for our replacement clothes.

In this state of absolute hopelessness, of being completely alone within the great mass of people, naked and freezing, something happened that I had no longer believed in. Suddenly – as if a miracle had happened – I heard the voice of my sister somewhere right behind me. I looked around. Was I hallucinating? Had my brain not been able to cope with all the terrible things that had happened in the short time since our arrival? Did I hear voices that weren't even there? I couldn't discover Aranka in the rows of all those bald naked women and girls. But my eyes kept on searching. There! That could be her! Yes, that was her! Our eyes met and at that moment we were running towards each other. We fell silently into each other's arms, pressed and hugged each other, held each other so tightly that nobody could separate us. Bare naked and bald we had hardly recognized each other. We promised each other at that moment that one of us would never leave the other's side again.

Luckily none of the guards had noticed this scene, we looked over to the SS men who were busy with other things, and so we had the opportunity to change places so that we were now standing next to each other in the row of five. I was no longer alone! Aranka was here with me again, my heart leapt with joy in this absolutely hopeless situation. Aranka, my beloved sister, to whom I could cling to, was finally near me again! Someone who could give me support and orientation. Together we could be strong, together we would be able to get through it all, no matter what was still to come.

Eventually we were handed out some completely tattered clothes. I got a totally torn dress. Underwear and stockings were not given to us at all. With red paint they painted a big red stripe on the back of our 'robe' in order to identify us. Then the humiliating welcoming procedure in the camp seemed to be finally over and all I was hoping for now was to find a place where I could at least breathe a little and recover from the strains together with Aranka.

Figure 33: Hungarian Jewish women standing in front of a barrack for roll call after they have been shorn, disinfected and newly clothed. Archive Yad Vashem.

18

Roll Call, Hunger, Thirst

But resting was not yet a possibility. On the contrary. We marched off and arrived after a short march at Camp B III in Birkenau. The Birkenau camp consisted of large wooden barracks, which were not even finished when we were taken there. There were no furnishings in the barracks, no beds, not a single piece of furniture, only the bare floor. In one such barrack we were crammed together with about 800 women. The wooden floor was to become our quarters for the next time. In the total confinement there was hardly any room for us to lay down or even turn around when we had found a place. And if someone had to go to the latrine that was next to the barrack at night, he could only go out stepping on and between the other bodies. The place that had previously been fought for with great effort was of course no longer free when you returned, and you had to find another place with the greatest of difficulty. So I spent the first night in our new 'domicile', tightly wrapped with my sister on the floor in this indescribable narrowness. Despite the traumatic experiences of the past days, I slept deeply and firmly, without thinking about what would await me the next day.

Figure 34: The wooden barracks in Birkenau. When Blanka arrived, they were not yet completely finished. Archive Auschwitz-Birkenau.

Although the following day would decide whether my young life would continue at all, because it was the day when the lie 'Yes, I will even turn 17 soon!' saved my life.

Yet what was actually left of my life after the separation from my parents and after I had come to this inexpressible place? I am here in a place and it seems to me like I am on a strange, uninhabitable planet. Human creatures, who have nothing human in their nature, determine our life. How will things continue on this planet? What will become of us? What do these aliens have in mind for us?

These questions move me and all the others. We are full of fear. Over and over again I discuss these questions with Aranka. We sometimes try, if we succeed, to chase away the negative thoughts by talking about home, our parents, our brothers and sisters and imagine what it will be like when all the bad things are left behind us. We envision images of a beautiful future. In this way, step by step, we find a little courage to face life again. We encourage ourselves that we will get through it all together. Yes, together we can manage it...and then we will meet our parents again, whom we both long for so much.

Life in Birkenau – if one can even use the term 'life' for it – is a struggle, every day, from the first to the last minute. Every day we have to get up at three in the morning, shouting and commanding, get out of the barracks and line up in rows of five for roll call. They count us all the time. Back to front, front to back. Just to harass us. It's bitterly cold in Auschwitz at dawn, even in June. We tremble in our pitiful clothes and press close against each other whenever possible to keep us warm.

During the day, however, it is unbearably hot. Shadow is nowhere to be found. In the whole camp there is no tree, no bush, not even a patch of grass. It is really like another planet, a strange, hostile world, unexplainable to my mind as a child. The sun burns our necks, our faces, our ears and especially the completely unprotected bald heads.

We hardly get anything to eat. How are we supposed to survive here even a few days? It is not enough to live, but just enough not to die of hunger. We are vegetating. The morning after the roll call at six o'clock we get a substitute black coffee brew, the 'Auschwitzer Schwarze-Tränke'. At least it's a bit warm! In addition we get our daily bread supply. However, the bread cannot be compared with what is commonly known as bread. It is an indefinable solid mass that tastes awful bad. At first I refuse to eat it, it is too disgusting for me, but Aranka insists on eating it because we have no alternative – except to starve. In the first days some of our comrades refuse to eat their rations, but soon they have no other choice if they want to live. It is the only food that at least fills us up a little, and soon everyone eats it completely in the morning to satisfy the first hunger of the day. Sometimes, but only very rarely, we get some jam or a piece of margarine with the bread during the day. However, by the time we receive this distribution, we have already eaten our little piece of bread.

We have to eat the so-called lunch standing in rows of five. The first in the row gets a bowl with a broth that is cooked from dried vegetables, pieces of branches and a mixture that does not reveal what it actually is. The bowl, full of broth, should be enough for all five in the row. We have to divide it up ourselves. There are no spoons. So everyone drinks two or three sips from this shapeless bowl and then passes the food on to the next person. The procedure continues until the bowl is empty. We are far from being fed with this. Hunger is our constant companion and we learn to live with it. It happens that we find a piece of potato or something similar in the broth. Then, of course, our joy is great. We take a sharp stone and divide the piece into five parts, so that everyone has something of it.

But much worse than the hunger is the thirst. I can barely handle it and at times it almost drives me crazy. The drought constricts our throats during the heat of the day.

A ditch runs through the camp with stinking water like broth. Many of us simply can't stand the thirst anymore and drink from the contaminated water. Knowing that this can have terrible consequences for them in their already weakened condition, they do it nevertheless. Many perish miserably, nothing can help them anymore, nobody except us prisoners takes care of them. Sometimes I ask myself whether they have chosen the better way, because their suffering has come to an end. But I want to live!!! I am still so young, I still have everything ahead of me, I also want to get to know the beautiful sides of life! In situations like this, Aranka and I are always talking to each other, encouraging us to live, telling us stories, imagining the future.

Occasionally a tank truck comes and brings us drinking water in two rusty basins made of sheet metal. We can hardly wait for this moment and rush to the fresh water. The sadistic chauffeur – an SS soldier – chases us away from the water every time. Then he takes some filthy cloth out of his car and calmly washes his car with our drinking water, while we can hardly stand it anymore waiting for the moment of redemption. Finally he finishes his procedure and we rush to the water. The fact that this is now dirty from washing the car does not bother us much. But still the driver has not tortured us enough. His sadism is boundless. He takes a walking stick out of the car grabbing some of us by the neck dragging them into the water with it. I'm lucky I can barely dodge it He is enjoying every minute of it laughing like a madman. Every time he comes back to bring us water – unfortunately much too rarely – the ritual is the same. We all endure it because we know: this sickening sadist is the only one who can quench our unbearable thirst.

In the course of the next few weeks we lose more and more weight and become weaker and weaker. Many women become sick, our weakened bodies are susceptible to any infection. Some die of typhus or simply of weakness. An increasing number of women are sorted out during the regular selections and sent to the gas chamber. Yes, it is now clear to all of us what happens to those who are selected. At first it is just a rumour that quickly gets around. Other prisoners are whispering to us that we shouldn't call in sick, because otherwise we would be gassed. We don't want to believe something unthinkable like this is really possible and despite knowing better, we are still under the illusion that it is all just scare-mongering. Our brains couldn't cope with anything else without despairing completely.

After five seemingly endless weeks with the same daily routines, consisting of arbitrariness, fear, desperation and threat, 18 June, my fifteenth birthday, which I had been looking forward to so much just a few months earlier, is coming. I wanted to celebrate it with my schoolmates and with my family. My mother would have prepared a birthday cake, I would have received little presents and we would have all spent a happy day together. But now?

On my birthday we'd be woken in the middle of the night as usual. I am lying on the floor of the barracks with Aranka close to me and before Aranka can even say Happy Birthday and tell me her good wishes, we have to go outside. Hours of roll call in the freezing cold morning before I get my 'birthday coffee': Auschwitzer Schwarze-Tränke and a piece of dry bread. My birthday...another endless day in Auschwitz with humiliation and degradation. Only Aranka takes note of this day, which is actually special for me, and we try to imagine how it would have been to celebrate this day together with our parents and siblings. But we can't stand it for long without bringing tears to our eyes. Infinite sadness and despair overcomes me as I fall asleep that evening. I hold Aranka's hand never wanting to let go.

The next day, male prisoners who have already been in our camp from time to time arrive. They have to clean the latrine and now relentlessly enlighten us about Auschwitz: The selections serve to separate those who are fit for work from those who are not. Those who belong to the second group have been sentenced to death. Those who are selected are taken to the shower room, but from the showers there comes not water, but gas. Hundreds, even thousands, are actually killed in this way. The bodies are burned in a crematorium that runs at full speed day and night.

Now the purpose of the high chimneys is obvious: these are the chimneys of the crematorium, and the smoke that moves across the camp grounds and spreads an unpleasant smell are the death clouds of our friends and relatives. The thought of it takes my breath away: Auschwitz is nothing more than a huge slaughter house. Everything is set up to kill people, at neck-breaking speed and with no leftovers.

A thought keeps shooting through my head: Mother! Was she really supposed to...? No, she must live! But I can't suppress this thought any longer, until it also becomes a tragic certainty: Mother is dead. At first I can't talk about it with Aranka, we keep silent, both obviously have the same thoughts, but don't speak about it. Without a word we finally fall into each other's arms and let our tears flow. Thank God we still have one another!

19

Selection as Salvation

What's to become of us? What's happening next? Are we just waiting for our murder? We are aware of the fact that our physical condition is getting more and more miserable and it is only a matter of time when we will have to follow the path that our mother has already taken. Yet we want to live! We don't give up on ourselves, keep on telling each other stories about our home, envisioning a better future. If we lose hope, it is all over. It is the only thing that remains, the only thing that allows us to maintain our dignity as human beings. We want to live!

But every selection becomes an ordeal. Aranka and I live in constant fear of being separated. We try to hide our injuries. But that is almost impossible when we have to march naked, holding our clothes over our bodies, past Mengele and his henchmen. I try to hide my festering wound on my foot, caused by the completely torn shoes that I have to wear without socks. However, I cannot hide my body, swollen by sunburn, from these cynical and sadistic male eyes.

With all my strength I try to keep myself in such a way that I make a healthy impression on Mengele. We try not to lose our dignity completely and march past the brutes in a proud posture.

After seven weeks in Auschwitz, another selection takes place at the end of July, this time obviously on a very large scale, in which a larger group of Hungarian girls and women are selected – as I learn later, exactly a thousand. We pass, as so often, Mengele and his men. Trembling with fear we try once again to keep our composure and not to show our injuries. Will we succeed this time as well? Aranka and I stay close together as always, but still it is here again: the fear of being separated. Disparagingly we are looked at like cattle. Why do they look at us this time even more precisely than usual? Why are they looking at us more closely this time than before? The finger points to the right for Aranka, who is walking in front of me, and to my relief the finger points the same direction for me. We are among the thousand chosen – without knowing what this selection means, what the consequences will be for us.

We are led to a field near the camp, the sun is low, it is almost evening. But nothing more happens. I wonder what they're going to do with us. They leave us sitting in freezing all night long. Why? Is it time for us to go now too? But why not now? In the morning, when it was not completely bright yet, we were being chased into a building we immediately recognized as a decontamination station. We get the order to undress, then we have to go to the shower room. We wait for water – and suddenly the light goes out. Panic erupts, everyone screams and some try to break the windows. 'This is it, now we are going die!' Aranka and I desperately cling to each other, waiting to die. Suddenly the door is ripped open and the SS men are yelling: 'Should shut up and stay calm! The lights were switched off because of an air raid

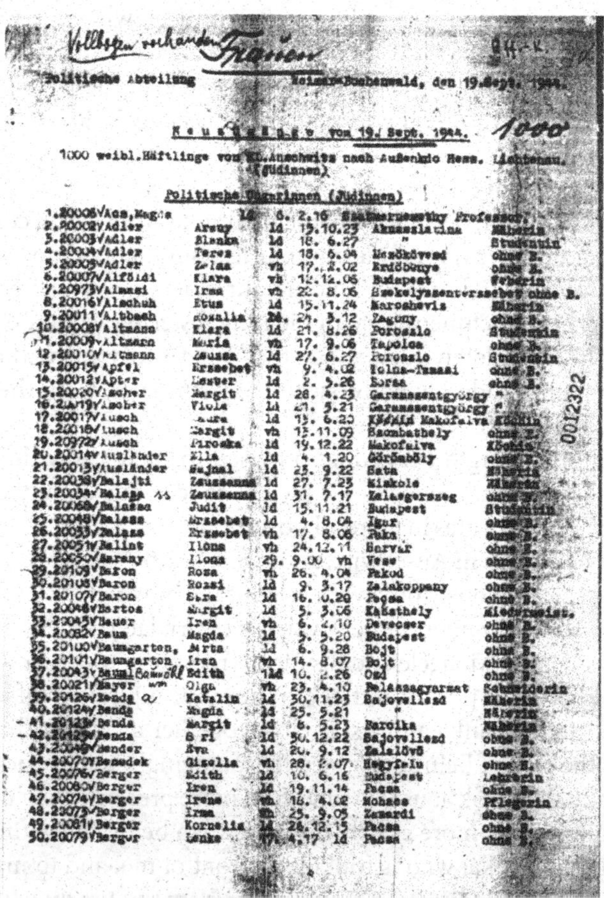

Figure 35: Transport list from Auschwitz to Hessisch Lichtenau, issued by the administration of Buchenwald concentration camp on 19 September 1944, after the women and girls had arrived in Hessisch Lichtenau on 2 August. In second and third place on the 17-page list are Aranka (Arany) and Blanka (with the wrong year of birth 1927) Adler. Archive Auschwitz-Birkenau.

Figure 36: Jewish Hungarian women in Auschwitz, selected for forced labour for the German armaments industry, ready for transport. Archive Auschwitz-Birkenau.

alert.' But I didn't believe them! The door closed and we were left behind completely rattled. Nothing happens until all of a sudden the light comes on again and finally – like a redemption – water actually flows out of the showers. We are alive! We can't believe it, but we really are alive! Full of joy we let the water flow over our tortured bodies. We have survived, at least for the moment.

Once we have showered, we are given new clothes. What on earth is that supposed to mean? It's strange, our totally worn out clothes are being replaced by something better. We all receive a new bag-like garment, which we still have to wear without underwear and stockings. Suddenly we're leaving. They're taking us to the train station. Again we are then penned in cattle cars, as on our transport from Hungary to Auschwitz, and once again we are heading towards an unknown destination, not knowing where we are going or what to expect there. 'If you want to survive, you have to get out of this hell,' I had heard it over and over again. And now, now we are leaving this hell. But where are we going and what will be the consequences? Anyway, I just can't imagine any place worse than this.

20

Hessisch Lichtenau – A Limited Paradise

On the 2 August 1944 we arrive in Hessisch Lichtenau after a long journey. We must have been a terrible sight when we were allowed to leave the wagons at Lichtenau station, exhausted and emaciated as we are. Upon seeing us at the station, our new camp commandant yelled in horror and indignation: 'We were supposed to receive workers, not skeletons. How on earth are these people going to work in the explosives factory?'

From the train station we are led by the SS men to a camp with wooden barracks, the Lager Vereinshaus, on the outskirts of the town of Hessisch Lichtenau. After a few minutes' walk we reach the camp. Fortunately the way is not far. Compared to Auschwitz, the camp seems almost like a 'paradise', at least at first we think so. Our pitiful condition leads to the fact that we are

Figure 37: The two photos show the barracks of the Hessisch Lichtenau concentration camp Vereinshaus on the outskirts of the city in 1952. The former camp barracks were used as a school during this time. Archive Freiherr-vom-Stein-Schule.

first given a rest period in the camp, during which we are fed a little better so we can regain our strength. After all, we should be able to work for the German war industry afterwards. We are glad to be able to work in a factory, because that is a chance for us to survive! In addition to the initially good nutrition we finally get underwear after a few days, even a spare pair. By all this we realize that they don't just want us to vegetate here, but that we are needed as workers. However, we are certainly not treated as humans here neither, which becomes more and more apparent in the course of the next weeks.

Our so-called 'paradise' is gradually crumbling, because we realize very quickly that working in the armaments factory is not only extremely difficult for us physically, but also poses a daily danger to our lives. We work in three shifts. At first, a train takes us from Hessisch Lichtenau to Fürstenhagen station, about three kilometers away. From there, we walk uphill, perhaps two kilometers, through a forest, passing through the factory gate to get to our workplaces. But the train from Lichtenau to Fürstenhagen doesn't come every day, so we must frequently walk the entire way to the factory. It takes us more than an hour to get there.

The long walk in rain, wind, frost and snow becomes more and more an agony for us, as we are insufficiently equipped despite the additional clothing. Our worn out wooden shoes are soaking up water, and later, when winter sets in, the snow sticks to them. The SS women who are guarding us on our march to the workplace do not allow us to stop and scrape off the snow, causing it to stick several centimeters high under the soles of our shoes. Some of us tap their shoes together to get rid of the snow and warm their feet just a little bit. But whoever tried to get rid of the snow was beaten by the overseers or chased by their dogs. All of us were scared as hell by the German Shepherd's of the overseers and especially me. They were beasts standing in front of us with baring teeth whenever the guards ordered them to do so.

For me these daily marches are the worst part of my daily camp routine. I suffer more from those than I do from the most difficult work or even from hunger. During the summer, sand and pebbles trickle into the lumps of wood which we are wearing on bare feet. Stopping and shaking them off is impossible, it hails an immediate beating. My feet are sore all the time. In winter it is the lack of clothing, the cold and the wooden shoes without socks in which you have to rush up and downhill which torment us. Sometimes some just pick up their shoes and walk on barefoot. But even if our feet are bloody, we are still afraid to call in sick, because we can already sense what is waiting for those who become incapable of work. Later on our concerns turn out to be legitimate.

Figure 38: Main entrance to the explosives factory Hessisch Lichtenau. The concentration camp prisoners had to pass the guard house (left) every morning, after they had already completed a walk of one hour or more. On the right is the administration building of the factory (photo from the 1950s). Private Archive Dieter Vaupel.

Several times in winter my wooden shoes completely disappear in the high snow, I can hardly find them. My feet are so cold that I have no feeling in them anymore. It is not possible to walk such a long distance in these shoes without terrible torture. Every day we arrive at the factory, barely able to work. The factory supervisors must have noticed that as well. We are supposed to work for them and accomplish something! So after a while we get different shoes. Leather shoes, but they are hard as a bone and of poor quality and they don't make walking much easier. But at least they warm our feet a little.

We are suffering tremendously under the merciless SS women who are guarding us on our way to work. They are pushing us forward again and again regardless of our miserable health. Beating us all the way not to be late for another shift. Many times passing the centre of the small town of Hessisch Lichtenau with its picturesque half-timbered houses. Just like this scenery, I always envisioned the area where the German fairy tales of the Brothers Grimm played, which I knew from my school days. And indeed, many years later I learn that the area around Hessisch Lichtenau is called the 'Mother-Holle-Country' and that several Grimm fairy tales were written here.

During the long walk through the village, before and after work, we do not experience any sympathy, not a single human remark by the people of Lichtenau. They just pretend that they don't see us. But are we invisible? Yet we actually have to create an image of emaciated figures wrapped in rags that you can't just walk past. However, they really pretend as if the fact that we are walking by ragged, shaven and tormented is the most natural thing in the world. It is strange and I don't know what they feel and what is hidden behind their ignorance, whether it is real or whether they are motivated by fear. As we march to work, I keep dreaming of what it would be like to walk through this beautiful town one day, not as a prisoner walking on these streets, but free and with my head held high on the sidewalk, not knowing that this dream would come true.

21

Canaries

Our working hours in the explosives factory are ten and a half hours a day. We work in a three-shift rhythm, including Saturdays and Sundays. Occasionally, when we have finished our shift, we have to do more work on the factory premises – it is absolutely inhumane what is being asked of us! Plus walking to and back from the factory. If we have a night shift, which is really unbearable for me, they often let us work additionally in the camp during the day, so that four hours of sleep are an absolute exception.

The work we have to do every day is not only extremely hazardous, but also physically exhausting. It feels like we always have to be where the most unpleasant work has to be done: making explosives, clearing up the factory site, working in the forest, loading and unloading railway wagons, loading and unloading at the factory, ground work such as digging trenches and shafts. We are slaves without rights only alive to do such work – until we drop. And it happens daily that some of our camp mates collapse at work.

Some of my few friends are off even worse off than Aranka and me, they have to physically work even harder each day at a construction company that apparently has jobs to do for the explosives factory. Martha is one of them. She is tough and has a strong will, but even she says it is almost unbearable. When she comes back from work, she always lies completely apathetic, like a dead body on her sleeping place – as long as she is left alone. Her hands are red and sore and full of blisters and scratches.

Most of us women and girls, including Aranka and myself, are employed at the exceptionally dangerous filling stations and crushing plants. We are responsible for filling and assembling grenades, mines, bombs and other projectiles. Aranka, me and a few other fellow prisoners are responsible for delivering the blanks on wagons, filling these bomb casings with the hot, liquid explosive trinitrotoluene (TNT), sealing the bombs, screwing them together, stamping numbers, packing, loading them onto trolleys again and transporting them. Of course all this is done under strict German control. We are monitored at every step of the work and some of us are driven to work repeatedly. But fortunately not everyone in the factory is like that.

Figure 39: In the casting house, which was part of the filling station, the liquid explosive TNT was filled into the blanks with casting vessels. The concentration camp prisoners were not provided with protective clothing like these two women. German Federal Archive Berlin.

I often have the task of carefully stirring the hot explosive to be filled into the grenades with brass sticks so that it cools down evenly to prevent air bubbles from forming in the explosive. A hard, ice-like skin forms on the surface. This must be cracked open constantly with the stick. I have to inhale the bitter-tasting, unhealthy vapour constantly. Sometimes I am numbed by it and I usually only come to my senses when the hot explosive splashes into

Figure 40: Blanka had to carry out this work. The hot, liquid mass in the bombs had to be carefully stirred with a brass rod so that it cooled down evenly and no air bubbles formed. The women were exposed to the poisonous fumes without protection. Painful injuries were caused when the TNT splashed up. German Federal Archive Berlin.

my face and burns my skin. Meanwhile my face is full of bigger and smaller burns. My sister is really worried about me when she sees me with all these wounds. I try to hide them as much as possible from the guards, because after the experiences of Auschwitz I am still afraid of being sorted out as unable to work.

In addition, I am forced to do other work that is far beyond the capabilities of a 15-year-old girl. Occasionally, after mounting, I have to grab these grenades weighing almost 65 pounds at the end of a conveyor belt and carry them for a short distance. I often severely injure my hands while doing this kind of work. I don't want anyone to see my festering wounds, I am trying to conceal them from other people's eyes, only Aranka knows about them. She comforts me and inspires me with new courage. She's such a marvellous sister. 'Where does she find her strength?' I wonder sometimes. She is almost like a mother to me, she helps me whenever she can without complaining about her own situation. She provides the warmth I need in this cold world that surrounds me, in order to have a chance to continue living and working day by day, to get through it all, not to surrender, not to despair.

Needless to say, the rest of the women and girls who work with me at the same site are no better off. Aranka spends the whole time filling the grenades, which is more and more damaging to her health, because she is permanently exposed to the toxic fumes. She is frequently coughing, and as her little sister,

I am very concerned to see how she, despite her psychological strength, is becoming physically weaker.

Sarah, a comrade, has to remove a boiling chemical mass from a large cauldron with a simple bucket and carefully pour it in. Several times she suffers burns as the hot liquid splashes back. But she has to continue working, mostly without medical care. She has never received leather aprons as protection, as the German workers receive them, nor have the other Hungarian women. We are slave labourers, no more no less, we don't need protection! Those who die are simply replaced. Sarah must also suppress her pain and camouflage her wounds. She knows too well if she calls in sick and cannot continue working, she will be declared 'unable to work'. We all know, but do not express, what will happen afterwards.

Some of us are also working at the punching machine, where the empty shells have to be marked with information. The date must be pressed inside the grenade using the punching machine. The women's hands are full of metal splinters, due to the fact that they don't have any gloves or leather aprons to protect them. To avoid an infection, they are advised to wait until the splinters eject themselves. Even so, this is very painful. Others, who stack and pack grenades, can hardly handle the heavy weights because they are simply too weak for it. It often happens that the grenades slip out of their hands. A few weeks after our arrival, a girl from our barrack dropped a grenade on her foot, but she had to continue working without medical help until the wound had healed by itself.

Some fellow prisoners are used as 'horses'. They have to pull flat, four-wheeled rail wagons, fully loaded with grenades, through a tunnel of about 110 yards. After this stretch, the wagons pass through a heavy iron door leading to the outside and finally enter a storage room where they have to be unloaded. A few days later, the railway wagons are loaded with the grenades from this warehouse. Everything needs to be done very quickly. The women working at this station are constantly driven to hurry. One such grenade weighs a good 45 pounds and the women and girls who are deployed here must learn to handle two at the same time.

Handling the poisonous explosives is a high additional burden for our already extremely weakened bodies. Sometimes the sickness creeping up on me is unbearable at work. Hunger, an empty stomach, exhausting work, extreme working hours and toxic steam…how can we cope with that without consequences? As if it's not enough our skin and hair turns greenish-yellow to red from working with explosives. After a few weeks at the filling station we all look like that. The beginning of heavy liver damage as I was diagnosed later. As if they wanted to mock us, we are called 'canaries' by the other factory workers, regardless of our pitiful condition.

22

Children, Go to Sleep

Sometimes I'm fortunate and I'm sent to the department in which the empty grenade and bomb shells are prepared for filling. There I get to know Helga, a young German woman who doesn't work willingly in the factory either. Like thousands of other women, she was obliged to work in a factory essential for warfare because of the shortage of labour – almost all the men were at the frontline. She noticed my pitiful physical condition and took great pity on me. Helga helps me wherever possible. She always comforts me, talks to me, although this is strictly forbidden to her and she has to expect the most severe punishments for it. I am thankful that I have learned the German language so I can talk to her.

Sometimes she tells me, 'Lie down in a corner, you poor little girl, and rest a while. I'll be watching over you and warn you if anyone comes'. I find myself a place on those empty shells and in a few seconds I'm fast asleep. It's good to have such a person near me! So there are humans among the wolves after all. Experiencing this helps me even more than the short rest I get while sleeping.

She brings me food, small bites, again and again without having much to eat herself. Maybe she has a little sister I remind her of, I'm thinking. Considering all the coldness around us, I'm absorbing all of the warmth she's giving. A song which she's singing to me quite often reveals that she is really not feeling well herself: 'Oh damn, you god damned employment office, you banished me to Hessisch Lichtenau, where the sausage portions weigh seven grams, and where hunger begins after dinner.' Soon I know it by heart, and we sing it quietly together, always being careful that nobody notices our friendship.

Obviously there are still people who can remain human even under the prevailing circumstances, even if it is only for minutes or hours that the good inside them breaks free. Such situations, as I experience them with Helga, show me that even among the German workforce there are men and women who empathize with us, who are linked in humanity with us and our suffering. They are also extremely afraid. They are not allowed to communicate with us or to contact us in any way. However, if someone wants to help us, it is possible, but you have to overcome the constant fear for this moment. Just like Helga does.

Other camp comrades also talk about having contact with German workers and with workers from other nations, from whom they receive something to eat. All of these contacts take place secretly, of course, usually in a few unobserved minutes or seconds. Rona tells me about a foreman named Hans, who tries to make things easier for the women wherever he can. Sometimes during the night shift when he realizes how tired and how exhausted they are, he tells my comrades: 'Children, go to sleep. I'll go on alone.' So they seek a place to sit or lie down and rest for a while. It is precisely the friendly choice of words using 'Kinderchen' (little children) that makes them feel so well, after the countless humiliations they have had to endure. It turns us into human beings again.

Occasionally I have to help loading the grenades into railway wagons near the filling station. There we meet French and Dutch forced labourers who are supposed to work with us. When we are not being watched by supervisors, they show us how to damage the detonators on the bombs in a way that makes them useless. Whenever we have the opportunity to do so in the future, we do so. In doing so, we are aware that we are putting our lives

Figure 41 Loading ramp of the explosives factory Hessisch Lichtenau. Here the slave labourers had to load bombs, grenades and mines into wagons. Here, together with French forced labourers, they repeatedly rendered bombs ineffective and carried out sabotage. Photo by Dieter Vaupel.

at risk. We know what happens if we get caught. Of course we are constantly monitored by German workers, but there are still unobserved moments that we take advantage of. Especially in the period after December 1944, we have better opportunities to sabotage without being discovered, because the controls are diminishing steadily.

For us, these operations are of enormous importance, and we are willing to take the looming risks. The thought of being able to contribute a little to Germany's defeat in the war, even in our situation as slave labourers in a large armaments factory, builds us up, strengthens our will to survive and helps us to persevere. We envision how many lives can be saved by every bomb which doesn't ignite. We take courage from it! We return proudly to our camp after work on such days without even noticing how badly we do physically.

The forced labourers from France are also helping us wherever they can. They give us little things that we can use. Needles and thread, a bar of soap and a comb, which especially delights us, because we can finally comb our hair again which fortunately is growing back slowly. And even more importantly, they'll whisper the latest news about the war to give us courage. Nazi-Germany is more and more on the retreat and we are gaining new hope!

23

Easier Work?

In October 1944, alien SS men came to our camp. What are they doing here? I'm sure this can't mean anything good. Once again I seek the closeness of my big sister, as always in situations where I feel helpless and exposed. They say the men came from another concentration camp. We all fear a scenario that we know too well from Auschwitz and of whose significance we know: selection. All other women and girls are just as concerned as we are. Yet once again, we do not know what is to come.

I observe within our barrack how the Kapo woman Manci Pal approaches some of her camp comrades with whom she is very close. She is whispering something to them. I wonder what she whispers. Might it have something to do with the arrival of the SS men? Manci knows everything. And most of the women know to survive here you have to get along with Manci. But she has her circle, her group of women, and for most of us it is impossible to belong to them. I got used to the fact that there's a hierarchy among the inmates, too.

We don't have much time to think about it after these men have arrived at the camp. All the sick are initially chased out of the infirmary by the strangers as well as our guards and placed separately, regardless of their physical condition. How cruel! Some of them can't make it on their own and must be supported by their comrades. Then we are all called to roll call. The camp commander, Schäfer, and his deputy Zorbach, whom we all hate and fear, gather in front of us. Also the camp elder Manci and the prisoner doctor Luciana Nissim, a Jewish woman from Italy, are standing there. Luciana! All female prisoners appreciate her deeply. She looks very serious, almost sad. She is often serious, because she is always busy. Yet she has such a good heart and helps us as much as possible, almost without medical resources. Apart from aspirin she obviously has no other medication at her disposal. A comrade who had suffered an injury at the punching machine told me that she had stitched her gaping wound with a sewing needle and thread. She then wrapped the wound with a paper bandage. For me Luciana is a heroine! How many of us she had already helped and always made sure that we did not have to stay too long in the sick bay. She knows the dangers very well, because before she came to us, she was a camp doctor in the hell of Auschwitz.

The foreign SS men initially remain in the background. Schäfer, as camp leader, has the task of explaining the situation to us. He says in a calm, expressionless voice that it has become clear that for some people the work in the explosives factory is apparently too hard. So they decided to make their lives easier. He is asking for those who consider their work too hard to step forward. They could get an easier job in a cardboard box factory. Family members who want to stay with their relatives could also come along. Spontaneously I twitch my arm – lighter work, yes, that is tempting! That would be something for Aranka and me! The daily work in the factory while handling the grenades and bombs is getting harder and harder for me and also Aranka is not as strong as a few months ago. Who knows how long we'll be able to stand it. But instinctively I am keeping my arm down for now. Many others come forward. I look at Aranka questioningly. But she shakes

```
SS Kommando              Hessisch Lichtenau, den 29. Oktober 1944
Lager Vereinshaus
Hessisch Lichtenau



         W a f f e n  SS
Konzentrationslager Buchenwald

Abtl.........

Weimar - Buchenwald


Betrifft: Rücktransport von 206 nicht arbeitseinsatzfähigen
          jüd. weibl. Häftlingen nach Auschwitz-Birkenau.

     Das hiesige Außenkommando sendet in der Anlage die Personal-
listen von dem am 27. Oktober 1944 zurückbeförderten 206 nicht
arbeitseinsatzfähigen jüd. weibl. Häftlingen nach Auschwitz -
Birkenau.

                                   SS -Sturmscharführer
```

Figure 42: The document proves what was at first only rumoured among the women and girls in the camp: 206 women who were not fit for work were transported back to Auschwitz-Birkenau. The text read: 'Subject: Transport of 206 Jewish women prisoners who were not fit for work back to Auschwitz-Birkenau. The local Außenkommando is enclosing the personnel lists of the 206 Jewish women prisoners who were not fit for work and who were deported back to Auschwitz-Birkenau on 27 October 1944.' Archive Auschwitz-Birkenau.

her head almost imperceptibly and I can see from her eyes that she is thinking.

'There's something wrong with this!' It'll become obvious much later how right she is. It's a good thing she's kept her healthy distrust of whatever comes from the SS people. You can't trust their promises. How many times have we experienced until now that people are trying to trick us again and again. I recall the situation in Auschwitz when I stepped forward to be with my mother. That could have meant my death. And now – Aranka and I sense – it's that kind of situation again.

But the longing of many girls and women to finally be given an easier job and no longer have to deal with the heavy bombs is enormous. Some of them simply cannot manage the work anymore. How many I had already seen who simply faint out of weakness at work or while standing at the roll call area! I take a look at the women, who are now being assembled separately into a group. How miserable most of them look! You can hardly call them humans anymore. Emaciated, hollowed cheeks, dark eye sockets. Many of them, despite their best efforts, can no longer stand up straight, some have to be carried by others. A pile of pitiful human misery. Right now I just pray so much for their sake that it is not a lie and they are giving them easier work.

But to be honest, I am extremely skeptical and I am fearing the most terrible, because earlier I was closely watching who our block elder was talking to. I can't find any of her confidantes in this group. That makes me really suspicious, because if she knows anything that might help to relieve her friends, Manci has always taken advantage of that. If there really was easier work at the other place, then her friends would be there too.

The group of women is gradually growing, because now all those who have been in the sick bay are being added to it. They are being dragged and pushed to the opposite side, sometimes with brute force and accompanied by a lot of shouting. So after all my guess is correct: a selection – even if Schäfer told us otherwise! It doesn't take long and the group of women – 206 in total, as I learn later – is led out of the camp by the foreign SS men in the direction of the railway station. Facing an uncertain future.

During the next days and weeks the rumour persists that the group was not led to an easier work, but was transported back to Auschwitz. Sad certainty about the fate of our camp comrades reaches me many years later, as I myself get my hands on a copy of a list at the end of the 1980s, with all the names of those who were selected. They were indeed transported back to Auschwitz and were sent directly to the gas chambers without being registered on arrival, without mercy. None of them survived.

Once again the SS has betrayed us with a brutal insidious lie. Easier work in a cardboard box factory...we all longed for it so much.

24

Eyes, Faces, Bodies Like Humans

The conditions in the camp are getting worse and worse – especially since a few weeks before the selection a new SS man, the already mentioned Zorbach, arrives at the camp. Rumour has it that he was sent from Buchenwald because our camp leader Willi Schäfer was not sharp enough, not cruel enough, to us. He had remained at least a little bit of a human being throughout all the things he had to do. Sure, he was an SS man and had to follow the rules and regulations, which he did, but he was not vicious. Zorbach, who from now on becomes Schäfer's deputy, is terrible, he is a beast. He tortures us not only physically but also mentally whenever he can. He also has a negative influence on the other SS men and manages to get the worst, the most brutal, the most inhuman out of them. In the course of time, he brings the entire SS guard staff up against us even more! Schäfer is powerless against him – he can do absolutely nothing, the power balance has shifted.

From now on, nothing in the camp is predictable. Arbitrariness may strike us at any time and any place. Zorbach's 'favourite words' are so mean, so vicious, as I have never heard them before in my life. He is constantly yelling at us about trivial things: 'I'm gonna tear your assholes up to your collars!' This feeling that arises is indescribably sickening. We already know that we are only numbers in this system, they took away our name, and they want to take away our dignity as human beings. But now we are only called the 'dirty Jews' and the 'dirty Jewish whores', as if we had no names and no families.

So we all have to watch how our prison mate Esther is getting kicked in her belly and beaten bloody by an SS man, who is called 'Stepdaddy', just because she didn't stand as still as he wanted her to during an hour-long roll call. And this is just one of many incidents. In some situations I simply have to look the other way. I can't watch it. I can't cope with it inside my child's soul.

Henceforth every opportunity is taken, also by the other SS men and women, to torture us, to beat us and literally smash our souls to death. Meanwhile, they have made a sport out of it, who is the most brutal and most barbaric. It is not only the men who are sadists, the women are no less brutal.

Mrs Bohle is particularly bad at beating, insulting and demoralizing us time and again. When air-raids became more and more frequent towards the end of the war and the hope for liberation began to sprout in us, she tried to take away all our hope by screaming: 'You're all going to be killed anyway, whether we win or lose the war!

In my mind of a child I wonder sometimes whether these people are human or not. How can you do this to others, treat someone like this? I am thinking they have eyes, faces and bodies like humans, but do not behave like humans at all.

Although on our arrival in Hessisch Lichtenau and during the first weeks I still had the impression that everything here was different and much better compared to Auschwitz, I now feel more and more like on a strange, completely uninhabitable planet. Vicious aliens around me that I can't understand. I want to go back to my little childhood planet with human laws! Back to Käsmark, Aknaszlatina or Leva. We never had it easy there, I had not been born on the sunny side of life. But I was protected from arbitrariness and malice. I want to return to the comfort of my parents' home, I long so much for my mother and father, who I miss endlessly. Fortunately at least Aranka is by my side. Otherwise I might have given up on myself a long time ago.

However, still not all members of the SS are taking part in the humiliations and abuses. There are a few who remained human after all, not being vicious monsters. One of them is Annemarie, with whom I personally have little to do. But Martha, who is supervised by her at work on the construction site, is telling us about her secretly: 'Annemarie shared her lunch with us today and she allowed us to go into the heated barrack a couple of times to get warmed up.' Even the little fat SS man, Neumann, is different. He is a naturally benevolent man and helps us more often, occasionally he secretly brings leftovers from the staff kitchen to us. People like Annemarie and Neumann give us at least a tiny bit of faith in this preposterous world.

During the course of time the other living conditions in the camp also become increasingly worse. The food rations, which until now consisted of water soup with turnips or white cabbage, some slices of bread, sometimes a few pieces of potatoes or a little jam, are now becoming scantier. Additionally, the barracks, which were initially overheated in winter, are now no longer heated at all, because apparently the heating material has run out. All we have are thin blankets on our bunk beds and we are freezing miserably. Besides, our barracks are now full of bugs. The straw bags we have as mattresses are full of them. So we can hardly sleep despite the hard work that leaves us extremely tired. Of course this wears our already frail bodies out even more and deprives us completely of the vitality left. Even our food is covered with bugs and by now I not only know what a bug looks like but also what it tastes like.

From now on we find our shower rooms regularly locked, so we have hardly any chance for proper personal hygiene. We are told since we are pigs we don't deserve any showers at all, especially as we are not keeping them clean enough. In addition, the roll calls and the working hours are being constantly increased. I ask myself, when will all this finally come to an end? Aranka and I try to encourage ourselves once again, but we hardly succeed. We can't give up now! We have already survived too many terrible things! This shouldn't have been in vain.

The news of the advancing allied troops is reaching us in some way almost daily, and increasingly hope for liberation is rising. We are already making plans for our future, and in our minds, fantasy images are emerging of what it will be like for us. In any case, I want to continue my school education, I am eager for knowledge and eager to learn. And despite all the contradictory information, I still have trouble believing that my mother is supposed to be dead. I can't and won't comprehend it. I have one last spark of hope. Together we imagine in the most beautiful pictures how the reunion with our parents and our siblings Roszi and Deszö will be. This encourages us not to despair and to keep going.

25

Evacuation of the Camp

On 29 March 1945, while we were at work, SS men from our camp followed us to the explosives factory. They have orders to lead us back to our camp immediately. In the last couple of days we have already heard the gun thunder of the frontline from afar, so it was clear to us that the liberation troops of the Allies must be very close. We are full of hope that our suffering will soon come to an end, and so we are marching back to the camp on this day feeling a tremendous relief. We dream of being free again, that we will soon feel like humans again, whose dignity is respected. However, one never knows what Zorbach or some of his particularly sadistic SS friends might have in store for us. They notice our mood, of course, because we have gained new confidence and are now showing it because we all are longing for this suffering to end. But still they are trying to take away our hope and continue to humiliate us. Upon our return to the camp, one of the SS women yelled: 'Just don't think that you will be free. Once the SS have you in hand, they'll never let you go.'

A few hours later the time has come and the entire camp is evacuated in view of the increasingly loud gun fire in the west. Some camp mates are spreading the word that there was supposedly an argument between Zorbach and Schäfer about the fate of us prisoners. Schäfer wanted to avoid evacuation, he simply wanted to wait until the Americans would be in Hessisch Lichtenau and then hand over the camp to them. But Zorbach had other ideas. His goal was to clear the camp in any case and to flee from the advancing front. Finally he gained the upper hand, probably also because the command situation was on his side. If Schäfer had had his way, we could have avoided much more suffering that was to come during the next weeks.

Another rumour has been circulating for days. Apparently they are planning to kill us all by injection before the liberation troops arrive. But fortunately this doesn't prove to be true. Yet it shows that we are still completely at their mercy and how desperate our situation still is even in view of the approaching liberators. At any moment, an arbitrary action by the SS can put an end to our lives. Emotionally, we are constantly being tossed back and forth. Our emotional state oscillates between hope and fear...

We have to line up on roll call square, and the SS guards are driving us in rows of five to the train station. Their attitude towards us remains unchanged, we are still being pushed and yelled at, we are still the 'Saujuden'. We are squeezed together so tightly in the waiting cattle cars that you are only able to stand up straight without any chance to move. An unimaginably oppressive tightness! If someone only dares to lift his foot, he can hardly put it back. No one would willingly haul his cattle under such conditions. Once again we are facing a totally desperate situation. Once again we are crammed into cattle cars. Again there is a bucket for the emergency relief and another one filled with water for all of us. It feels like a recurring nightmare. Memories of the deportation from Hungary to Auschwitz are coming up inside me, anxiety and fear is spreading among all of us. I smell the sweat of the others, which is not only due to the oppressive narrowness and lack of oxygen. It is the pure sweat of fear. I squeeze myself very tightly against Aranka and realize how she struggles as well to hide the panic that is building up inside her.

In addition, our wagon is guarded by the most sadistic overseer Mrs Bohle. If there are witches, she is one! The greatest sadist among SS women. Already in the camp she never missed a chance to humiliate and degrade us, and she still maintains this attitude right now.

As we prophesy a better future to each other from the palms of our hands, facing the desperate situation, I can hear her sarcastically say: 'You still believe in future? That's ridiculous, they're already heating the crematorium for you!'

It is obviously their intention to take us to the concentration camp Weimar-Buchenwald, to which the Lichtenau KZ-Außenkommando is administratively assigned. This is probably the reason why Zorbach insisted so strongly on evacuating the camp in the face of Schäfer. After many hours of travel, with numerous interruptions, our train stops for a while on the railway track in Weimar. We read the station sign and Aranka comes to mind that in her school days she had heard of the great German poets Johann Wolfgang von Goethe and Friedrich Schiller, who came from Weimar. Where has Germany's cultural tradition gone in recent years? In any case, we have not noticed anything about the fact that we are in the land of great poets and thinkers.

After our train has stood on the railway track in Weimar for a few hours, we suddenly, to our greatest relief, move on. As it turns out in the course of the journey, we are heading for Leipzig. Again and again our train has to stop. Fortunately, these are opportunities to at least empty the miserably stinking latrine buckets – if we are allowed to. Nevertheless, the conditions in the wagons become more unbearable by the hour. The terrible narrowness, no possibility to lie down, it is almost impossible to stand. We only receive food and water very rarely. We become even weaker than we already were in the camp of Lichtenau. How is this supposed to continue?

Once the train comes to a complete standstill because the locomotive is obviously broken and cannot be repaired. It takes a day and a half until our train receives another locomotive as a replacement and the journey can continue. When the doors are being opened during another stop, we are finally allowed to get off the train. Of course we are sharply watched by the SS crew. Aranka and I lie down in the grass, even though the ground is still damp and cold at this time of year. It is a feeling of relief – even if only for a few minutes – to finally be freed from the confinement. But this feeling is suddenly shattered as gunshots are fired. Some SS men start shooting ferociously without warning. What's going on here? Are our guards losing their minds? Two women are hit, they die on the spot from the gunfire. Some of us are forced to dig a grave for them where they are simply thrown into. The situation leaves us extremely terrified, because obviously some SS people have become even more unpredictable by now. We are wondering how all of this will finally come to an end?

After five days of travelling by train, we reach Leipzig and are able to leave the wagons. From the station we are led to the camp Schönau. The camp is actually already fully occupied, with several hundred concentration camp inmates, like us Hungarian women who came from different camps. They are in a much better condition than we are. We assume that they obviously had an exceptionally good camp commandant. We get a really good meal in Schönau, without the everyday feeling of hunger right after the meal.

We can even take a shower. What a luxury! Then we are taken to the barracks, where we are allowed to rest in the bunks. We can hardly understand it. Rest! When was that last time? Immediately we feel a little more like humans again.

But our rest in the bunks will not last long. The very next day, 6 April 1945, the camp was attacked with bombs and set on fire by American low-flying planes. Within a few minutes, parts of the camp are on fire, some barracks are completely destroyed. The whole incident really happens within minutes. I was just sitting with my sister in one of the bunks on a straw bag when a detonator bomb shoots through the window of our bunkhouse and immediately lights a fire. We try to escape into the open, it is a terrible crowd, not all our comrades are getting out of the barrack in time.

Once we are outside, we repeatedly hear the explosion of the bombs and the desperate cries of trapped people. A total chaos develops. Outside we have no means of protection, only the SS men are allowed to use the shelters.

Has our last hour come? Again it is my sister who gives me hope through her closeness and her comforting words. At some point the bombing finally stops. Deeply sad we realize that several of our camp mates lost their lives in the fire. Nobody knows how many were killed. They have gone through so much in the past months, they had such high hopes for liberation. And now they are dying in the bombing raids of the liberation troops. How ironic...

A few hours after the bombing we have to line up again in rows of five and are led through Leipzig. To the both sides of the street it looks terrible. Leipzig has been bombed just recently and most of the houses are nothing but burnt ruins. We arrive at the Leipzig-Thekla camp, a men's camp, also a subcamp of Buchenwald, which is already occupied by many prisoners. After having suffered the bombing of camp Schönau, we are even more terrified by now. 'We want to survive and not die at the last moment,' keeps going through my mind.

In Camp Thekla we are at least reasonably well supplied and we can rest for a while. Here we stay until the American troops are within earshot just a few kilometers west of us. On 13 April, five or six days after our arrival in the camp, all inmates, including us the remaining slave labourers of Hessisch Lichtenau, are sent on a march that becomes a march of death for more and more prisoners the longer it lasts.

26

Death March

As usual we are lined up in rows of five. The guards are loading their luggage onto handcarts, which some of us have to pull in turns. The march begins. Where will this journey take us this time? What might be done to us? Which orders are given to our guards? They're heading east first. The roaring of the cannons and the clattering of the machine guns from the west are gradually diminishing. Along the way, other evacuation marches will join us. All heavily guarded by SS or German soldiers. We march day and night, occasionally we are allowed to rest. Obviously, the guards want to prevent low-flying planes from spotting the convoy. That's why we stay in hideouts, in barns, on farms or in dense woods.

We don't get any rations. We have to survive on plants that we find along the roadside. We drink from puddles or creeks. At a time when many of us started deeply believing in liberation, all of this adds to our suffering. We are led further and further east for days until we cross the river Elbe. The Russian army is literally coming towards us, the thunder of gunfire can already be heard clearly. Hope for liberation grows again for a few moments. But since the SS staff does not want to be captured by the Russians in any case, they let us turn around and we are marching back towards Leipzig.

Our 'life' only takes place outdoors, we are at the mercy of wind and weather, and have nothing to protect us. It is April, and it is still very cold, especially at night. Plus it's pouring constantly. But the hope for an end to our suffering allows me and Aranka to continue fighting for our lives. If we have the energy to do so, we will talk to each other, continue to make plans for our future. It helps us morally. But many of us are so weak that they can't go on. They are simply dumped along the roadside and shot. Brutally, ruthlessly, without mercy. Again and again we hear the rattle of guns. And we move on, not looking back...

Basically, we freeze and starve for two weeks straight. The blanket we have wrapped around us doesn't help much either. It is neither a real protection against cold nor against wetness. Little by little it rots away. The rags that serve as clothes never come off our body during the whole time so they stick to us. Most of the time we are totally apathetic, our legs only move mechanically. Sometimes I lose all hope of liberation. The death march

Figure 43: Death march: physically and mentally devastated, wrapped in blankets that offered hardly any protection, the concentration camp prisoners were still driven back and forth between the fronts in the last days before the end of the war. Photo by Benno Ganther, AKG-Images Berlin.

convoy is now increasing daily. Everyone is moving in the same direction. Thousands have now joined, waiting for death or liberation just like us.

In our misery, we continue to chew the grass or herbs we find along the way. Every once in a while, when we are allowed to rest, we can make a fire and warm ourselves a little. Aranka and I have a tin can that we fill with water to boil nettles. We drink the nettle broth as if it was a delicacy. But we move on quickly. We march past fields and potato acres. Some of us try to get to the fields to dig up some potatoes with their bare hands. But they are aware of how dangerous it is. Sometimes the SS people don't notice it, but if they do, they just shoot. Again and again our comrades die in the hail of bullets because they couldn't endure the hunger.

The paths we take are paved with dead bodies. Countless dead bodies. Everywhere. I can't take it anymore. It completely overwhelms me. It feels like my brain is shutting down, fading out all the horror surrounding me. My gaze is focused only forward, accompanying my legs to the rhythm of my steps. I, like so many others, have learned how to sleep while walking.

Sometimes we are trying to drag those who can't go any further with us, but we are too weak ourselves. Nevertheless we are trying, and sometimes it helps to be supported a little while. Despite our weak condition, some of the guards are still beating us. And we are constantly being chased forward. 'Just don't leave the convoy', I tell myself, because if I do, it hails kicks and punches or it might happen something even worse. The SS monster, Mrs Bohle, is unfortunately still by our side. Until the end she tortures prisoners with sadistic joy. I see how Golda, one of our fellow prisoners, is beaten by her until the SS woman claims that she is now tired of beating.

The frontlines are now approaching from both sides. Some of our fellow prisoners use the signs of disintegration during the final days of the march to flee, as our guards are becoming increasingly inattentive. Shall we try as well? I am talking to Aranka about it, who is still my greatest strength and constant protector during the death march. She refuses, because it is too dangerous to be killed by these guards who still show no mercy. What would have happened to me without my sister? Aranka is firmly convinced by now: liberation is near, we would make it. We don't want to put our lives on the line now.

There are further signs of the approaching liberation to be observed: More and more SS men are leaving the marching convoy. Every day there are less of them. And we haven't seen Commander Schäfer for days. Did he also 'heroically' escape like the others? At a rest I notice that several SS men are having their insignia cut off their uniforms, some are putting on prisoners' jackets and are simply running away.

27

Liberation: Human Wrecks, But We Live!

On 24 April 1945 we are taken to a barn for the night near the small town of Wurzen, east of Leipzig. All of a sudden the remaining SS-Crew is very friendly towards us, as we had never experienced them before. They are now tearing all their insignia from the jackets, under no circumstances should they be recognized as SS men. To our astonishment, we suddenly hear them say things like: 'We didn't mean to do you any harm!' or 'You know that we were only obeying orders.' What hypocrisy! Do they believe in that we will testify for them at our forthcoming liberation so that they might escape punishment? They are talking about us being their prisoners today, but tomorrow they will be prisoners themselves, and we will be free people.

The fate that awaits them now does not move our hearts. Are we to take pity on these ruthless people now, after they tortured us like this? We remain silent in order not to provoke these still unpredictable people in the end. Nevertheless, our inner joy is immense, knowing that the next day we shall finally be liberated and our suffering will come to an end. The SS is now talking quite openly about handing us over to the American army. We are asked to make white flags from our clothing. Is that meant to be ironic? How's that supposed to work? All we have on us are filthy rags! But anyone wearing anything that is even a little bit white tears off a piece and ties it to a stick or a branch. We don't want to be shot by our liberators at the end!

Early in the morning we leave the barn with our strange little peace flags. Uniformed Americans on motorcycles approach us and planes fly low over our heads. This is it, the very moment of our liberation. A moment we have been longing for, for an endless time of despair, suffering, fear, as well as hope. And now it is suddenly there, freedom.

Aranka and I sit down on the sidewalk exhausted and tired falling into each other's arms like so many others. We're alive! We made it! We have the feeling that we couldn't take any further step. But we are alive! From now on we are free, but we have no clue what it actually means for us to be free. Human wrecks, skeletons, emaciated, hungry, tired, penniless, no roof above our heads, what shall become of us? What are we supposed to do with our freedom anyway? It's a wonderful feeling to be free. Tears run down my face, tears of joy. Tears of relief. But also tears of sorrow. I feel joy but at the same

PARIS List 1102 B.　　　　　　　　　　　　BV
　　　　　　　　　　　　　　　　　　1st June 1945

List of Jewish women found alive in
concentration camp at WURZEN (Germany)

HUNGARIAN

NAME	H/WN	AGE	CONTACT
AUSCH Margit	Szombathely	36	
Mrs. APPEL Laszlo	Dombovar	43	Mrs Apfel Kolman Switzerland
AUSCH Piri	Kolozsvar/Cluj/	28	AUSCH Eugen New-York
AUSCH Laura	"	25	"
ADLER Aranka	Löve	21	
ADLER Blanka	"	18	
AFTER Peter	Borsa	16	
ASCHER Margit	Garamszentgyörgy	23	
ASCHER Margit	"	21	
ACS Magdelna	Eger	28	
ALTMANN Klara	Poroszlo	18	
ALTMANN Zsuzsa	"	13	

Figure 44: Document of liberation after a long suffering: 'List of Jewish women found alive...' with Blanka and Aranka Adler. Archive ITS Bad Arolsen.

time everything suddenly seems so hopeless. Totally overwhelmed by the emotional chaos.

At this very moment a group of American soldiers comes towards us, interrupting my thoughts. They ask if we are hungry. What a question! Everyone can tell! Of course we say yes. They are telling us to follow them. We're not far from the railway station in Wurzen. They lead us to a camp full of sugar bags very close to the train station. The crystal sugar sacks are made of paper. We are amazed! What an abundance! What a difference to sorrel, grass and nettles! The soldiers simply cut the paper bags with their knives and the sugar trickles down on us like a waterfall. We feel as if we were in a land of plenty. Not milk and honey flow everywhere, but inexhaustible amounts of crystal sugar! Each of us tries to eat as much of it as possible, including Aranka and me. Such a greed! We just can't stop. When was the last time we got some candy? We stuff our pockets full to the brim. The

American soldiers are happy about our enthusiasm and we thank them for showing us paradise. But how dangerous the sudden, intensive consumption of sugar can be, we realize a few days later, when many who had been there with us become very ill. The emaciated bodies could not cope with the incredible sugar shock.

From the sugar warehouse we are led directly to the barracks, where we are now temporarily accommodated. Finally we are able to take the clothes from our bodies for the first time! But along with our clothes, which have literally been sticking to us for two weeks now, our skin, just like snakeskin, also comes off. When I lay my clothes, or rather the decayed remainders of them, next to me, my sister discovers lice inside of them. How disgusting! She is very agitated, because lice are known as carriers of typhus. With the rags in our hands, we go straight down to the barracks yard to burn them. Since I don't have any other clothes yet and won't get them until later, I am standing completely naked in the yard of the barracks next to Aranka.

At last we are finally able to clean ourselves and we are given used clothes to put on. Unfortunately these clothes are of poor quality too. Nevertheless, at least we have something fresh to put on for now. We soon notice that the supply by the Americans is quite disorganized in all areas. I think they were not prepared for the condition we are in, that they would encounter such terrible looking skeletons. Once a day they come to our barracks with a truck full of food and clothing. They simply throw everything they have loaded off the truck. Nothing is thought out or planned. Those of us who are stronger get more, and those who are weaker get nothing.

So we who are among the weakest continue to starve. The only option left for us is to look for food outside the barracks. That's what we'll do. We walk through the town of Wurzen begging for food. If we can't get anything else, we'll plunder shops together. What other choice do we have? We've been starving for so long. Once we just tear down a big curtain in a shop and run away with it to our quarters in the barracks. So some of us girls will sew dresses out of the fabric. I know how to do it, I often watched my father at work. Even without a sewing machine and with improvised sewing equipment we are able to do this. So I sew together my first dress being a free woman. What a feeling to have a dress of my own, not some discarded rag. My dress of liberty! This is the dress in which I'll spend the next time. For the next two months it will be the only garment I own. But I am wearing it with pride!

After the official end of the Second World War on 8 May 1945, Wurzen is cleared by the Americans, it now belongs to the Russian occupied zone. For the time being we are allowed to stay in the barracks. We realize very quickly that the Russians, who are now looking after us, are much better organized for taking care of us prisoners. They immediately set up a kitchen for us, from now on there are regular food rations for every single one of us. Bread is always available. Every day at noon and in the evening they serve a good and satisfying meal for everyone. We feel that our lives are slowly returning to some sort of normality.

However, all of us girls as well as women are constantly afraid of rape, because some girls are abused by the Russian soldiers. It is beyond imagination that anything like this is happening in such a situation. None of us expected it.

After all, we are all just skeletons, and we still do not even feel like women yet. But the Russian soldiers seem to be so starving for women that they even rape the girls and women who actually don't look like women at all. So we have to live with a new kind of fear again, but fortunately Aranka and I are spared.

28

Return: Nothing Is As It Was

As we are still sick and weak, I am taken to a quarantine camp in Sagan in the south of Poland together with my sister, where we will stay for almost 40 days. We get medical treatment and they take very intense care of us with great effort. Finally, after many terrible experiences, we meet human beings again – no aliens, no monsters, no robots, no sadists.

People from many nations, who were kept in the camps by the German National Socialists, are accommodated here to bring them back to life. Gradually we are looking better again. Slowly we can feel like humans again. Our hair grows back and we become young women again. How good it feels to have young men suddenly courting us here in this place, taking an interest in us without being pushy. Especially the young Italians. There are even dance evenings in which we participate and which we really enjoy. How wonderful it feels. We are slowly trying to live a human life here again.

After almost six weeks Czechoslovakian buses arrive in Sagan and together with the girls coming from Czechoslovakia we take the buses to the Czech-German border. In the Czech border town of Nachod we even get a passport and some money. Now we can feel like full members of human society again!

From Nachod, everyone sets off on their way home. We separate from all the other women with whom we shared so many things, and Aranka and I are on our own from now on. We know that it is still a long way to our homeland, there are still almost 500 kilometers to Leva. How are we going to get there? At first we're puzzled. But somehow we make our way, although we hardly have a chance to use a train or any other means of transport. So we are walking most of the way towards our home. What else can we do? At least sometimes we are able to take the train in our direction for a while.

After a few days we arrive in Pressburg (Bratislava). From here it is not even 100 kilometers to Leva. But I can't go one step further. My feet hurt unbearably, for days the pain has been getting worse and worse. My legs are thickly swollen. It's a miracle I made it this far. We're lucky to meet two young men from Leva who have business in Bratislava. They're staying at a hotel and will put us up for the night in their room. They see how bad I am and give us their bed while they sleep on a sofa or on the floor. All night long one of them alternately tries to massage my legs a little and cool them down to give me some relief. But it does not get better, the pain does not stop and once again I am very desperate.

The next morning the two men try to find me a place in a hospital, and they manage to do so. It is a hospital that has been specially set up for former prisoners, because apart from me, many others suffer from the consequences of the terrible conditions in the German camps. I was diagnosed with a thrombosis in my legs. 'I am only 15, my life is just beginning', I think. But now that doctors and nurses are taking care of me, I am hoping for a quick recovery. I will stay alone in the hospital for the time being. Meanwhile, Aranka will look for our apartment in Leva and see if our father has already arrived there. We hope so much that he – like the two of us – will have survived all the horrors of the past year.

As Aranka comes back to Bratislava after a few days I am feeling better again and the swelling has gone down. I am glad that she is coming to pick me up! But she brings sad news, since she is telling me that we don't have a home anymore. Our apartment is occupied by strangers, she reports. It is saddening us deeply and we start crying, as we have not done for a quite a while during the hard times we've been through. Now we may cry again. The last months we always had to stay very strong in order not to collapse completely. Now we can let our emotions go again.

We were so full of hope to be able to return to our home and now strangers have simply taken possession of our house, apparently even with the approval of the Hungarian authorities. Now we are away from the foreign, uninhabitable planet, but our old little planet, our home, is now uninhabitable for us as well. Does everything still conspire against us? Where are we supposed to live? Aranka had no choice but to find a place in a home for the homeless in Leva. Depressed and sad we take the train from Bratislava back to Leva. During the train ride none of us speaks a single word. So what will be our future?

When we arrive in Leva, Aranka makes sure that I will be accepted into the shelter together with her. After all we are given a roof over our heads. We are free now, but what does this newfound freedom mean for us? We don't know what to do with our freedom here. We do not have a job. We are completely broke. What we have left is the hope that perhaps our father survived in a labour camp. But we don't even know if he survived Auschwitz. And if he really did, where was he taken from there? So we wait for him every day in Leva. We ask everywhere if anyone knows anything about him, if anyone has heard from him. He was a little younger than our mother, only 47 years old and we still hope so much that he will be standing before us soon. But nobody can help us, nobody knows anything about him. Nevertheless we are still full of hope.

Until one day a Jewish doctor from Leva visits us in our home, who has survived the horror himself and has just returned. He brings the painful news that we no longer need to wait for our father. He had already died in his arms in December 1944. He had been struck by a terrible illness. In the concentration camp Dachau he had to do forced labour and, the doctor tells us, every day he had to carry heavy bags of cement to different floors without having a chance to shower or clean himself in any other way after work. As a result, the cement powder had gradually settled into his skin pores, where it combined with the sweat. This prevented oxygen from being transported through the skin, which practically suffocated him.

We are trying to imagine what a horrible death it must have been for him and it truly breaks our hearts in pieces. It hurts so deeply, to have this sad certainty of knowing we will never see him again. We never had the chance

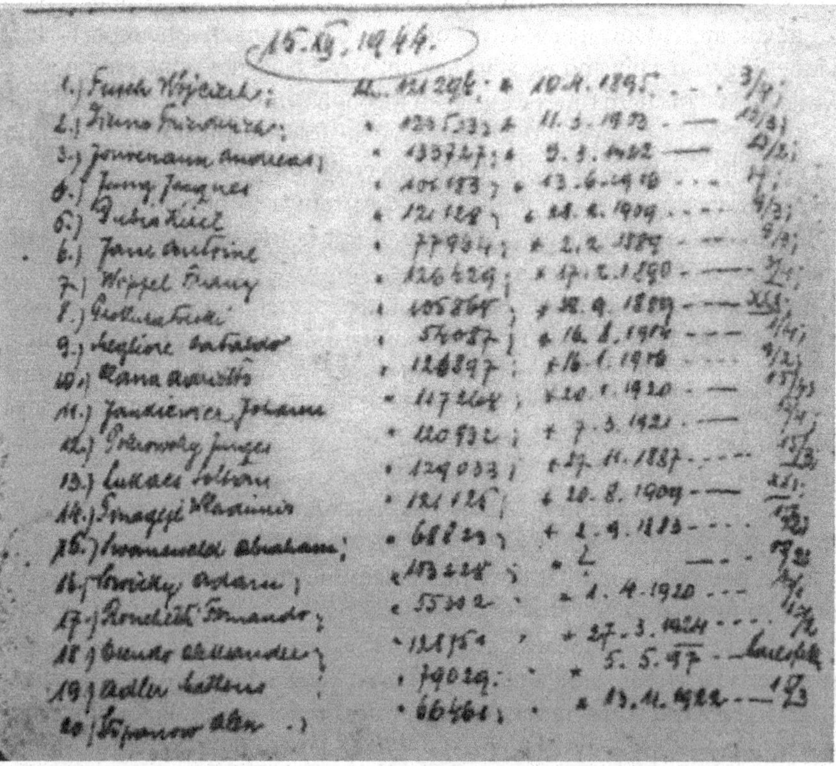

Figure 45: The book of dissections and the book of the dead of the Dachau concentration camp document the death of Mathias Adler. Archive ITS Bad Arolsen.

to say goodbye. For days we are paralyzed with grief, unable to think clearly. All our hope is crushed. Once again we feel lost, without any perspective. We are already all alone anyway...and now forever without a father. Yet it's not only the sorrow about our own future that paralyses us. We pity our father so deeply. The imagination that he suffered so terribly at the end of his life won't let us go. He never had it easy in his whole life. He constantly had to fight for his and for all our lives, in Aknaszlatina, Käsmark, Leva...in Dachau his strength was no longer sufficient.

After we had to accept this further heavy blow of fate, and we slowly return from the rigour of grief into the world, we are hoping and praying that at least our oldest sister Rosalie survived in Budapest. Life must go on somehow for both of us! We have already heard that many Jews were able to survive in the Budapest ghetto because, contrary to Adolf Eichmann's plans, they were no longer deported to Auschwitz at the end of the war. Because the war was almost over, most of them were fortunate and were spared the hell.

Coincidentally, we heard that someone from our town wants to go to Budapest because he has some business to do there and wants to meet his relatives. So we ask him to look for our sister. That won't be easy in such a metropolis. But he promises to do so. He will do everything possible to help us. We'll give him her last known address and hope he might discover something.

On his return, he reports that he didn't find her there. But he was told that she is alive and where to find her now. Furthermore, to our greatest joy, we also heard that our brother Deszö has already returned from the labour service a while ago. After all, there's finally something to be really excited about again! We are full of hope that we can hold them both in our arms again sometime soon.

Deszö didn't have an easy fate either. He and his comrades were supposed to go west first. But since he was stricken with typhus, they just left him behind. So he had to struggle on by himself, being seriously ill. He literally crawled on all fours because he was so weak, but his will to survive was huge. He's a fighter too, like Aranka and me, and he doesn't just give up. He dragged himself to a hospital in a small town near Budapest, and little by little he recovered. From there, as I learned later, he moved directly to our sister Roszi.

One day at the end of July 1945, as I am outside at the well in the courtyard of our home washing my clothes, my brother Deszö is suddenly standing before me. We look at each other, hugging each other wordlessly, but with pure joy in our hearts. Somehow he found out that this is our new home in Leva. Just as we were looking for him, he was looking for us. 'I

Figure 46: Blanka as a 20-year-old in 1950. Private Estate Blanka Pudler.

actually hardly doubted that any of you would ever come home,' Deszö said after a while of silence. 'Word has gotten around about what happened to the Jews deported from Hungary to Auschwitz. I'm so overwhelmed that you made it!' Now he had come from Budapest to pick us up: 'You need a new home! Pack your things and come with me to Roszi and her husband, they have prepared a place for you.'

He doesn't ask about our parents. I think he can sense that this – our reunion – is a great moment of joy, over which no dark shadows should lie. Only much later, after we have been living in Budapest for several weeks, does he dare to ask his questions, and we have to share the sad answers with him.

Figure 47: Blanka with her husband Janos, whom she married in 1950, and her daughter Agnes, who was born in 1952 (photo 1962). Private Estate Blanka Pudler.

We gather our few belongings in our home in Leva and travel together with Deszö to our sister in Budapest who, like her husband, welcomes us into her home with a wonderful warmth. Now Aranka and I finally have the feeling of security again, the feeling of having a family and a home. We are so grateful that the four of us at least stayed alive, even though we are still mourning our parents very much.

At first there is no chance for Aranka and me to stand on our own two feet. We don't have any money to be able to afford our own room. We are very grateful to Roszi and her husband for taking us in. But I still haven't given up my biggest desire to continue school. It is so important for me. I want to advance in life. At school I always had so much fun learning and I still want to know so many things! I dreamt of this again and again in Auschwitz and Hessisch Lichtenau. This hope for the future has contributed to my survival. It has always given me new courage.

But unfortunately the greatest dream of my life cannot come true because of our social situation. My brother-in-law makes it very clear to me that it is not possible to continue to go to school. I myself cannot afford to go to school at all, as I am penniless. I cannot expect my brother-in-law to support me as well. With all good will, but his income is simply not sufficient for that.

Figure 48: Meeting of the former Jewish forced labourers in 1987 at the invitation of the local history workshop and the city of Hessisch Lichtenau on the grounds of the former explosives factory. Blanka Pudler is the fourth from the left in the photo. Photo by Dieter Vaupel.

Well, what choice do I have? I have to get a job and go to work trying to stand on my own two feet as soon as possible. This causes me a tremendous heartache, because I was really hoping to continue my studies. But I will not give in, I swore to myself! Whoever survives Auschwitz, forced labour and the death march at the age of 15 has learned to fight, not to resign and to always find new hope...

Epilogue
Words by Blanka Pudler

It took us years to come to terms with the murder of our parents, the decay of our home, and to create a new home for ourselves. I still often have nightmares about our cruel past that we shared.

I haven't been able to talk about my past for a very long time. I have tried with all my strength to repress my memory, hoping to forget. But I couldn't.

I never thought I would find so many German friends in Hessisch Lichtenau, the place where I suffered so much.

Figure 49: Blanka in 2007 with students of the Drei-Burgen-Schule Felsberg. Photo by Dieter Vaupel.

I decided to no longer keep silent about my terrible experiences as a Holocaust survivor. Even though it is painful and the wounds are torn open again and again, I want the young generation to know what we had to go through.

Today I believe that to speak is no longer a need, but a duty.

I feel obliged to speak because I am personally affected again. My daughter is married to a man from Nigeria. My grandsons – half Jewish and half African – must be able to resist hatred already as children.

I have decided to speak as long as my strength lasts, and thereby contribute to ensure that something similar to Auschwitz can never happen again.

I feel obliged to speak before you about my fate, to warn you of intolerance and hatred of minorities. It's terrible where this is leading. I want to make a contribution to prevent something similar to Auschwitz from happening again.

Figure 50: Blanka with students of the Freiherr-vom-Stein-Schule Hessisch Lichtenau in 2008 on the grounds of the former explosives factory. Photo by Dieter Vaupel.

List of Illustrations

Figure 1: Old City Hall, Market Place, Hessisch Lichtenau 2019. Photo by Tourist Information Hessisch Lichtenau.

Figure 2: Spangenberg Castle ruins, 1949. Private Archive Dieter Vaupel.

Figure 3: Building #313, the Denitrierung or Denitrification Building. Photo by Christel Bukowski.

Figure 4: Building #379, the Verladerampe or Loading Ramp. Photo by Christel Bukowski.

Figure 5: Skeleton of the Boiler House. Photo by Dieter Vaupel.

Figure 6: Students, map in hand, walk past #567, Toilet House. Photo by Dieter Vaupel.

Figure 7: Students in Press Building #367, Hirschhagen. Photo by Dieter Vaupel.

Figure 8 Max Mayr at Buchenwald, as drawn by a fellow prisoner. Private photo from Max Mayr published in Jörg Kammler und Dietfried Krause Vilmar (Herausgeber/ Editor): *Volksgemeinschaftund Volksfeinde. Kassel 1933-1945* (Kassel: Hesse GmbH 1984), p.363.

Figure 9: German workers, Camp Waldhof, 1943. Private Archive Dieter Vaupel.

Figure 10: Posing for a photo on Heinrichstrasse behind Lager Vereinshaus barracks, 1943. Private Archive Dieter Vaupel.

Figure 11: German employees, Hirschhagen, early 1940s. Private Archive Dieter Vaupel.

Figure 12: Dutch men and German civil servant girlfriends, Hirshhagen, early 1940s. Private Archive Dieter Vaupel.

Figure 13: Memorial Inscription, site of former Lager Vereinshaus Hessisch Lichtenau, 1986. Photo by Dieter Vaupel.

Figure 14: Left to right: Iósza Ignácz, Klara Bohm, Ibolya Méth, Magdalena Kornfein, Henriette Szepes. Photo by Dieter Vaupel.

Figure 15: Jean Eclàche with Ibola Mèth and the translator. Private Archive Dieter Vaupel.

Figure 16: Some of the Jewish women who attended Haifa reception, 1987. Private Archive Dieter Vaupel.

Figure 17: Jewish survivor taking down inscription on Memorial Stone, 1987. Photo by Gregor Espelage.

Figure 18: Luciana Nissim and Martha Frank on bus to munitions factory. Private Archive Dieter Vaupel.

Figure 19: Magda Kornfein in press building explaining her work to Dieter Vaupel, 1987. Private Archive Dieter Vaupel.

Figure 20: Walking tour with survivors and students, Judith Isaacson front left, 1987. Private Archive Dieter Vaupel.

Figure 21: Tunnel-like entrance to a building in the munitions factory, 2016. Private Archive Dieter Vaupel.

Figure 22: Human chain to honour the women and girls of Lager Vereinshaus, 2019. Photo by ExtraTip Werra-Meißner.

Figure 23: Alida Scheibli and Dieter Vaupel at reading for documentary. Photo by: Reiner Sander.

Figure 24: Rieke Bauer as Blanka being marched from camp to the munitions factory. Dieter Vaupel Documentary 2019.

Figure 25: Marilen Schäfer and Lea Achler following route of Jewish workers from camp to factory. Dieter Vaupel Documentary 2019.

Figure 26: Blanka Pudler in 2008 in Hessisch Lichtenau at the memorial stone that was placed on the former camp grounds in 1986.

Figure 27: Blanka as a pupil in the German primary school in Käsmark. Private Estate Blanka Pudler.

Figure 28: The only photograph Blanka kept of her family: 1932 in Käsmark Blanka sitting between her parents Mathias and Eszter Adler, maiden name Pollak, behind her from left Dezsö, Roszi and Aranka. Private Estate Blanka Pudler.

Figure 29: Blankas' class at the State Middle School in Leva in June 1943, one year before her deportation to Auschwitz. Blanka in the back row, sixth from the right. In the centre of the front row is her beloved class teacher Maria Kovacs, next to her the headmaster. Private Estate Blanka Pudler.

Figure 30: Deportation of Jews to Auschwitz in Reichsbahn cattle cars where 80 to 100 people were crammed into one car. Archive Auschwitz-Birkenau.

Figure 31: Arrival in Auschwitz after a three-day journey in the cattle car. Aranka Adler was among those photographed in front of the carriages. She can be seen on the left-hand side of the photo wearing a headscarf between mothers with children. Archive Auschwitz-Birkenau.

Figure 32: Selection at the ramp in Auschwitz. Archive Yad Vashem.

Figure 33: Hungarian Jewish women standing in front of a barrack for roll call after they have been shorn, disinfected and newly clothed. Archive Yad Vashem.

Figure 34: The wooden barracks in Birkenau. When Blanka arrived, they were not yet completely finished. Archive Auschwitz-Birkenau.

Figure 35: Transport list from Auschwitz to Hessisch Lichtenau, issued by the administration of Buchenwald concentration camp on 19 September 1944, after the women and girls had arrived in Hessisch Lichtenau on 2 August. In second and third place on the 17-page list are Aranka (Arany) and Blanka (with the wrong year of birth 1927) Adler. Archive Auschwitz-Birkenau.

Figure 36: Jewish Hungarian women in Auschwitz, selected for forced labour for the German armaments industry, ready for transport. Archive Auschwitz-Birkenau.

Figure 37: The two photos show the barracks of the Hessisch Lichtenau concentration camp Vereinshaus on the outskirts of the city in 1952. The former camp barracks were used as a school during this time. Archive Freiherr-vom-Stein-Schule.

Figure 38: Main entrance to the explosives factory Hessisch Lichtenau. The concentration camp prisoners had to pass the guard house (left) every morning, after they had already completed a walk of one hour or more. On the right is the administration building of the factory (photo from the 1950s). Private Archive Dieter Vaupel.

Figure 39: In the casting house, which was part of the filling station, the liquid explosive TNT was filled into the blanks with casting vessels. The concentration camp prisoners were not provided with protective clothing like these two women. German Federal Archive Berlin.

Figure 40: Blanka had to carry out this work. The hot, liquid mass in the bombs had to be carefully stirred with a brass rod so that it cooled down evenly and no air bubbles formed. The women were exposed to the poisonous fumes without protection. Painful injuries were caused when the TNT splashed up. German Federal Archive Berlin.

Figure 41: Loading ramp of the explosives factory Hessisch Lichtenau. Here the slave labourers had to load bombs, grenades and mines into wagons. Here, together with French forced labourers, they repeatedly rendered bombs ineffective and carried out sabotage. Photo by Dieter Vaupel.

Figure 42: The document proves what was at first only rumoured among the women and girls in the camp: 206 women who were not fit for work were transported back to Auschwitz-Birkenau. The text read: 'Subject: Transport of 206 Jewish women prisoners who were not fit for work back to Auschwitz-Birkenau. The local Außenkommando is enclosing the personnel lists of the 206 Jewish women prisoners who were not fit for work and who were deported back to Auschwitz-Birkenau on 27 October 1944.' Archive Auschwitz-Birkenau.

Figure 43: Death march: physically and mentally devastated, wrapped in blankets that offered hardly any protection, the concentration camp prisoners were still driven back and forth between the fronts in the last days before the end of the war. Photo by Benno Ganther, AKG-Images Berlin.

Figure 44: Document of liberation after a long suffering: 'List of Jewish women found alive...' with Blanka and Aranka Adler. Archive ITS Bad Arolsen.

Figure 45: The book of dissections and the book of the dead of the Dachau concentration camp document the death of Mathias Adler. Archive ITS Bad Arolsen.

Figure 46: Blanka as a 20-year-old in 1950. Private Estate Blanka Pudler.

Figure 47: Blanka with her husband Janos, whom she married in 1950, and her daughter Agnes, who was born in 1952 (photo 1962). Private Estate Blanka Pudler.

Figure 48: Meeting of the former Jewish forced labourers in 1987 at the invitation of the local history workshop and the city of Hessisch Lichtenau on the grounds of the former explosives factory. Blanka Pudler is the fourth from the left in the photo. Photo by Dieter Vaupel.

Figure 49: Blanka in 2007 with students of the Drei-Burgen-Schule Felsberg. Photo by Dieter Vaupel.

Figure 50: Blanka with students of the Freiherr-vom-Stein-Schule Hessisch Lichtenau in 2008 on the grounds of the former explosives factory. Photo by Dieter Vaupel. www.dietervaupel.jimdofree.com

Bibliography

Buergenthal, Thomas: *Ein Glückskind. Wie ich als kleiner Junge Auschwitz überlebte und ein neues Leben fand(A lucky child. How I survived Auschwitz as a little boy and found a new life).*Frankfurt: Fischer Verlag, 2007.

City of Hessisch Lichtenau (ed.): *Themenweg Hirschhagen. Von einer der größten Sprengstofffabriken des Dritten Reiches zum Industriegebiet (Thematic trail Hirschhagen. From one of the largest explosives factories in the Third Reich to an industrial area).*Hessisch Lichtenau.

City of Hessisch Lichtenau (ed.): *700 Jahre Hessisch Lichtenau. Ein Beitrag zur Heimatkunde 1289-1989 (700 years of Hessisch Lichtenau. A contribution to local history 1289-1989).* Hessisch Lichtenau, 1989.

Espelage, Gregor: ‚*Friedland' bei Hessisch* Lichtenau(*'Friedland' near Hessisch Lichtenau).* Volume II: *Geschichte der Sprengstoffabrik Hessisch Lichtenau (History of the Hessisch Lichtenau explosives factory).* Published by the city of Hessisch Lichtenau in 1994.

Espelage, Gregor & Vaupel, Dieter: *700 Jahre Hessisch Lichtenau – Ein ergänzender Beitrag zur Heimatkunde.Rüstungsproduktion in ‚Friedland'* (*700 years of Hessisch Lichtenau – a supplementary contribution to local history. Armaments production in 'Friedland').* Die Fabrik Hessisch Lichtenau zur Verwertung chemischer Erzeugnisse. Witzenhausen: Ekopan-Verlag, 1989.

Freiherr-vom-Stein-Schule: *Erinnern – aber wie? Wie in Zukunft mit der NS-Geschichte in Hessisch Lichtenau umgegangen werden soll(Remember – but how? How to deal with Nazi history in Hessisch Lichtenau in the future).*Documentation of the project-week from 7-12.9.1987. Hessisch Lichtenau, 1987.

Hirschhagen Project Group: *Hirschhagen. Sprengstoffproduktion im Dritten Reich(Hirschhagen. Explosives production in the Third Reich).*Kassel and Wiesbaden: Hessian Institute for Educational Planning and School Development, 1991.

Jessen, Jürgen / Geschichtswerkstatt Hessisch Lichtenau (ed.): *Wie es war. Zeitzeugen des Holocaust in Schule und Öffentlichkeit.* (How it was. Holocaust eyewitnesses in school and in public). Witzenhausen: Ekopan-Verlag, 1994.

Magyar Isaacson, Judith: *Seed of Sarah: Memoirs of a Survivor*. Urbana: University of Illinois Press, 1991.

Magyar Isaacson, Judith: '*Freut euch, ihr Lebenden, freut euch*'. *Erinnerungen einer ungarischen Jüdin.* ('*Rejoice, you living, rejoice*'. *Memories of a Hungarian Jewess)*. Neu-Sokol, Gerda (ed.), Berlin: Hentrich & Hentrich, 2010.

Mark, Elke: *Kanarienvogel (Canaries)*. Book and film about Blanka Pudler. Cologne: Prima Print GmbH, 2008.

Moreimi, Eva: *Hidden Recipes. A Holocaust Memoir*. Minneapolis: Second Gen Press, 2019.

König, Wolfram/Schneider, Ulrich: *Sprengstoff aus Hirschhagen. Vergangenheit und Gegenwart einer Munitionsfabrik (Explosives from Hirschhagen. Past and present of an ammunition factory)*. 2nd ed. Kassel: University library 1987 (= Nationalsozialismus in Nordhessen, Volume 8).

Levi, Trude: *A Cat called Adolf*. Ilford: Vallentine Mitchell, 1995.

Levi, Trude: *Did you ever meet Hitler, Miss? A Holocaust Survivor Talks to Young People*. London & Portland, Or: Vallentine Mitchell, 2003.

Stone, D.Z.: *No Past Tense: Love and Survival in the Shadow of the Holocaust.* London & Chicago, IL: Vallentine Mitchell, 2019.

Pudler, Blanka & Vaupel, Dieter: *Auf einem fremden unbewohnbaren Planeten.Wie ein 15-jähriges Mädchen Auschwitz und Zwangsarbeit überlebte (On a Strange, Uninhabitable Planet. How a 15-year-old Girl Survived Auschwitz and Forced Labor)*. 2nd ed.Bonn: Dietz-Verlag, 2019.

Vaupel, Dieter: *Das Außenkommando Hess. Lichtenau des Konzentrationslagers Buchenwald 1944/45 (The external command Hess. Lichtenau of the Buchenwald concentration camp 1944/45)*. A documentation. 1st /2nd ed. Kassel: University Library 1984 (= Nationalsozialismus in Nordhessen, Issue 4).

Vaupel, Dieter: '*Unauslöschbare Spuren*' - *Zwangsarbeiterinnen der Dynamit AG berichten nach mehr als vierzig Jahren*('*Indelible Traces*' - *Dynamit AG forced laborers report after more than forty years)*. In: 1999. Zeitschrift für Sozialgeschichte des 20. und 21. Jahrhunderts, issue 4 / 1988, pp. 60-74.

Vaupel, Dieter: *The Hessisch Lichtenau Sub-Camp of the Buchenwald Concentration Camp, 1944-45*. Published in: Randolph L. Braham (ed.): *Studies on the Holocaust in Hungary*. Columbia University Press 1990, pp. 194-237.

Vaupel, Dieter: *Spuren die nicht vergehen. Eine Studie über Zwangsarbeit und Entschädigung (Traces that don't go away. A study of forced labor and compensation)*. Kassel: University Library 2nd ed. 2001 (= Nationalsozialismus in Nordhessen, Volume 12).

Vaupel, Dieter: *Materialien für den Unterricht: Auf einem fremden unbewohnbaren Planeten (Materials for Teaching: On a Strange Uninhabitable Planet)*. Bonn: Dietz-Verlag, 2019.

Index